Women According to Men

The World of Tudor-Stuart Women

Suzanne W. Hull

AltaMira
PRESS

A Division of Sage Publications, Inc.
Walnut Creek • London • New Delhi

For information address:

AltaMira Press
A Division of Sage Publications, Inc.
1630 North Main Street, Suite 367
Walnut Creek, CA 94596

SAGE Publications Ltd.
6 Bonhill Street
London EC2A 4PU
United Kingdom

SAGE Publications India Pvt. Ltd.
M-32 Market
Greater Kailash I
New Delhi 110 048 India

Printed in the United States of America

Library of Congress Cataloging-in-Publication Data

Hull, Suzanne W.
    Women according to men: the world of Tudor-Stuart women /
by Suzanne W. Hull
        p. cm
    Includes bibliographical references and index.
    ISBN 0-7619-9119-0   ISBN 0-7619-9120-4 (pbk.)
    1. English literature—Early modern, 1500–1700—History and criticism. 2. Women—England—History—Renaissance, 1450–1600—Historiography. 3. Women—England—History—17th century—Historiography. 4. Women—England—Books and reading—History—16th century. 5. Women—England—Books and reading—History—17th century. 6. English literature—Men authors—History and criticism. 7. Women—England—Conduct of life—Historiography. 8. Women in literature. I. Title.
PR429.W64H87   1996
820.9'352042'09031—dc20   95-50244
                                                                                          CIP

96 97 98 99 10 9 8 7 6 5 4 3 2 1

Interior Design and Production by Labrecque Publishing Services

Cover Design by Julia Hilgard Ritter

Cover Illustrations:
WOMAN IN SCOLD'S BRIDLE OR BRANKS, from *Englands Grievance Discovered* by Ralph Gardiner (London, 1655), p. 110, by permission of The Huntington Library, San Marino, Calif.
WOMAN RIDING MAN, title page of *Brideling, Sadling and Ryding . . .*, (London, 1595), by permission of The Huntington Library, San Marino, Calif.

Icon:
WOMAN WITH BASKET, *Ornatus Muliebris Anglicanus* by Wenceslaus Hollar (London, 1640), plate 26. By permission of The Huntington Library, San Marino, Calif.

Table of Contents

About the Author

Suzanne W. (Sue) Hull is the author of *Chaste, Silent & Obedient: English Books for Women, 1475–1640*, published in 1982 and reissued in paperback in 1988. It was reviewed favorably in the United States, England, and Switzerland and continues to be widely cited. *The Library* said of *Chaste*, "This well-written and well-produced book is a pleasure both to read and to use." An American journal called it "a uniquely wonderful study for all seasons, for all audiences."

Mrs. Hull was for fourteen years the first and only woman to serve as a principal officer of The Huntington Library, Art Gallery, and Botanical Gardens. She has served in leadership roles in a number of community and nonprofit institutions in the Greater Los Angeles area, including the presidency of the Los Angeles YWCA. She was a founder of the ongoing Huntington Women's Studies Seminar and is now a consultant or member of the advisory board of the Women Writers Project at Brown University and The Early Modern Englishwoman: A Facsimile Library of Essential Works.

Mrs. Hull holds degrees from Swarthmore College and the University of Southern California. She is the widow of an attorney and mother of three adult children.

Women According To Men

or

A True Recitation of
Instructions on How to Live
in an Orderly and More Perfect Manner,

WRITTEN BETWEEN 1525 AND 1675 BY MEN,

*Secure in the Knowledge of their Superior Learning,
for the Benefit and Guidance of all
Wives, Daughters, Mothers, Widows, Maidens,
and other Untutored Females in England.*

Together with Diverse Recipes and Solemn
Directives, Set out by the Same and Other Such Learned Men,
to be used by Females in their 16th– and 17th–Century
Households as in Preparing of Food and Pharmaceuticals,
Caring for Babies, Raising Daughters,
and Learning Correctly to Dress their Bodies and Souls
with Proper Clothing and Humility

Here adjoined together by one

SUZANNE W. HULL

A Matron of the Twentieth Century

Who offers forth for the Readers of these Curious Male
Quotations Sundry Expoundings to Place Them, with Speculation
and Wonder, in the Context of that Earlier Time.

*Thus Respectfully Presented for Publication
in this World of Continuing Gender Confusion,
Anno Domini 1996*

Preface

*T*he goal of this book is to provide an *introduction* to the world of English women from 1525 to 1675, using the written words of men of that time. It was an era recorded, in print, almost exclusively by men. More than 99 percent of all publications were by male authors.

Much of this period, Early Modern England, falls within the reign of the Tudor-Stuart monarchs and includes the English Renaissance. Early Modern literature boasts a large body of nonfiction—how-to-live manuals, recipe books, marriage guides, sermons, prayer books, solemn essays, and volumes discussing both the good and evil inherent in women. This literature repeats what society told women, in other ways, about their roles from birth to death. The books explain for us—as they did for literate women of the time—the limitations placed on the female sex as well as the broad extent of their domestic responsibilities. Men's views molded society; their books help to show what that society wanted from its women. Whether they present an accurate picture of the women is the difficult question.

The quotations in this book are taken directly from original sixteenth- and seventeenth-century books that discuss women and their activities. In their original form, the books followed few spelling or punctuation rules. To make the quotations more understandable, I have modernized spelling and, to a large extent, punctuation. I have not altered titles, however, since early books are generally known and catalogued under their original, idiosyncratic form. Most of the rare books can be found in the magnificent collection of early English books at the Huntington Library in San Marino, California. Many are available also in other major research libraries, including the British Library in London, the Folger Library in Washington, D.C., the Newberry Library in Chicago, and university libraries at Harvard, Yale, and (in England) Cambridge and Oxford.

For anyone wishing to delve more deeply into these old books and their topics, I offer a bibliography at the end of the text. It is lightly annotated where titles are not self-explanatory. I have also listed secondary sources that help in understanding the early books.

With the growing interest in women's studies, more of the old books are being resurrected in print, on microfilm, or on computer disk. For those unable to access any of the rare book libraries, I suggest three steps. First, learn whether the book has been newly reissued by checking *Books in Print* in any library or bookstore. (Some reprints are noted in the bibliography section of this book.) Second, contact University Microfilms International, Ann Arbor, Michigan 48106—or get in touch with major public and university libraries—for film versions. Third, for the rare books and journals *by women* (and there are some, though relatively few were published within the time period covered here), contact the Women Writers Project, Box 1841, Brown University, Providence, Rhode Island 02912, or *The Early Modern Englishwoman: A Facsimile Library of Essential Works*, in progress through Scolar Press, Old Post Road, Brookfield, Vermont 05036.

The lengthy and facetious frontispiece of this book is, in large part, a composite of many actual title pages found in the old books themselves. I include this imaginative page to give a taste of what was printed for a female audience between 1525 and 1675.

My appreciation must always go to the Huntington Library: first of all, for being there in all its excellence, and then for offering me a full research leave to work on this book when I retired as a staff officer. Thanks also go to Daniel Woodward and the late William Moffett, Huntington Librarians, who had the foresight (but not always the money) to acquire rare and reference materials that enhance the Huntington's strengths in women's history. I salute as well the Friends of the Huntington Library, who provide much-needed financial support to supplement the collections. My colleagues and I, in the relatively new field of Early Modern Women's History, are grateful for the reliable help these materials provide and for the collegial atmosphere the Huntington offers to all who use the collections.

My sincere and affectionate thanks go to indispensable friends, colleagues, and relatives who provided much-needed information or assistance, who read and critiqued the manuscript, or who simply listened to me by the hour. Among them are Charles Bell, Winifred and George Bond, Jean R. Brink, J. Kent and Carol Pearson Clark, David Cressy, Jane Donawerth, David Elliot, Marsha Fowler, Paul Hardacre, Edward Harnagel, Allison Heisch, Jane Hill, Elaine Hobbey, Maryanne Cline Horowitz, Anne Hull, Nancy and George Hull, Barbara Kanner, Bettyann Kevles, Arthur Kinney, Sara Mendelson, Elizabeth Pomeroy, Susan Kullman Puz, John Reid, Mary Robertson, Eleanor Searle, Anne Shaver, Hilda Smith, Frank Thistlethwaite, Betty and James Thorpe, Jenny and Ernest Townsend, Betty Travitsky, Ciji Ware, Susanne Woods, and Paul Zall. Most of all, to my son Jim Hull, I offer deep appreciation for the professional editing (and affectionate but stern encouragement) he gave to this undertaking. ❦

SWH
Pasadena, California

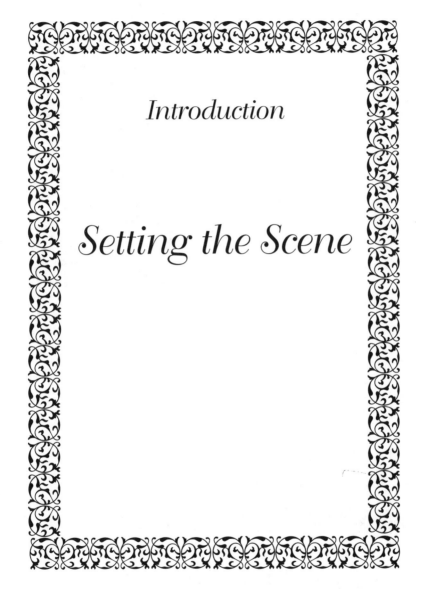

Introduction

Setting the Scene

Setting the Scene

What was it like to be a woman in Tudor-Stuart England, from the time of Henry VIII through the Restoration, roughly 1525 to 1675—

> when England was ruled for half a century by queens but women had almost no legal power;
>
> when marriage, women's main vocation, cost them their personal property rights;
>
> when the ideal woman was rarely seen and never heard in public;
>
> when the clothes a woman wore were legally dictated by her social class;
>
> when almost all schoolteachers were men;
>
> when medicine was prepared and water purified at home;
>
> when corsets were constructed of wood and cosmetics made of bacon and eggs;
>
> when only half of all babies survived to adulthood?

Opposite page:

Top MAN WRITING AT DESK, center segment of the frontispiece of *Gospelles of Dystaves* (London, ca. 1507). By permission of the Huntington Library, San Marino, Calif.

Bottom WOMAN READING AT LECTURN, from *Gospelles of Dystaves* (London, ca. 1507). By permission of the Huntington Library, San Marino, Calif.

Life was not the same throughout that 150-year period; after all, it included the English Renaissance, a time of great energy and creativity. But change did not occur at the breakneck speed of the twentieth century.

The Tudor-Stuart era is fascinating in part because it was so different from today. Yet it is also intriguing because some of its cultural attitudes still cast shadows on our modern society.

First There Was Man

The invention of printing was a boon to mankind. To womankind it was a boon—and a bane. Printing in English dates from about 1475. After that, more and more women learned to read, but men wrote and published nearly all the printed material during the next 200 years. And men produced dozens of directives—instructions—telling women how to live, work for, and obey the men in their lives.

Men wrote the marriage guides, the essays on how to raise daughters, and the discourses on women's place in the religious and cultural worlds of the day. They published recipes for cooking, home cures, and needlework designs. They prescribed suitable female education. They told women how to behave toward servants, speak French, write a respectable hand, and doctor to their families' wounds and illnesses. Their instructions even included how to conceive and give birth. Male writers taught what to wear (clothing suitable to one's rank), what to say (very little), where to go (few places other than home and church), and where to stand in the social hierarchy (below men).

Make no mistake: this was a patriarchal world. Father—or husband—knew best. At least, so said the books.

The very fact that these instructions were repeated over and over makes one doubt that all women followed them. But there was certainly a permeating norm that implied men were dominant and women, inferior. Saint Paul said as much in the Bible. His message, endlessly repeated during this period, was: "The head of every man is Christ; and the head of the woman is the man."[1] In a Christian country where the Bible was revered and taught from early childhood, such a pronouncement was as binding as law. In support of Saint Paul's edict, many men cautioned women to accept their inferiority; to be chaste, silent, obedient, and "shamefast" (bashful); and to remember that they were created after the man for his use and as his helper.[2] If there were ever to be equality between the sexes, declared one writer, it might possibly come in Heaven, but not on earth.[3] The lesson was: follow men's mores in life, and be rewarded after death. Those who ignored or flaunted the lesson faced the threat of a tortured afterlife in the nether regions.

The message came in various genres, from romances to prayer books, jest books to sermons, and even in a penmanship book. Around 1600, perhaps as few as 30 percent of men and 10 percent of women living in London could sign their own names.[4] The privileged few females with writing skills were to be taught only the simplest hand because women, "having not the best memories," had "not the patience to take any great pains, and [were] besides phantasticall and humorsome."[5] The author of that edict, Martin Billingsley, was a handwriting expert, purportedly the writing master to the future King Charles I.

Some books specifically addressed a female audience. The earliest English dictionary (published well before Samuel Johnson's famous work) announced on the title page that it was written for "Ladies, Gentlewomen or any other Untutored Persons."[6] Many other authors used title pages or dedications to direct their books to English women. Title pages tended to be lengthy—like the frontispiece of this book. They were the forerunners of dust jackets and served as introductions to the text. Extra copies could be printed as flyers and used as advertisements.

Basic to society, as asserted by most male writers, was the concept that women were inferior by nature and limited in aptitudes, and should stay at home and never speak in public. (Many men claimed women talked too much anyway.) They could "go abroad" (leave the house) to attend church or see to household matters or assist neighbors with domestic chores, but not much else. A woman could also, if deputized by her husband, carry out activities with or for him, as long as she never usurped his preeminent role. Or so said the instructions, though actual practice within the individual family may well have differed. Many of the arguments for obedience were tied to belief in a natural hierarchy in which women—being inferior—were expected to follow men's commands. It was argued that wisdom and leadership (as well as several other useful qualities) were rare in women.

Since women were expected to marry, bear children, and assist their husbands, and since men ruled the job market, it was difficult for females to make a living any other way than through marriage. Some women, often widows, did manage it. But most unmarried women worked in a home or carried on a business tied to domestic activities. It must not be forgotten that England in the Tudor-Stuart period was an agricultural, pre-industrial society where most people's work was centered in their homes or revolved around them.

The sex ratio created an ongoing problem as well. Beyond age sixteen, females tended to outnumber males in the cities and among the upper classes, creating an unbalanced population.[7] Despite deaths in childbirth, women seemed to survive disease, war, aging, and the other hazards of life more readily than men. It was a buyer's' market for men seeking wives. Men could lay down the rules for the behavior of their women.[8] And they did.

Because surviving books are authored almost entirely by men, they don't tell the whole story. They fail to get inside the minds and emotions of the women for a faithful description of their true lives and real beliefs. Still, we are dependent on written records for much of our knowledge about these Early Modern women. Perhaps women of the period didn't believe everything they read or were told. But the evidence suggests otherwise. Well-worn guidebooks, as well as frequent reference in women's journals to their own obedience to religious and cultural norms, suggest that most women accepted "common knowledge." This spanned many beliefs, from vital matters, such as how to conceive a child or behave as a proper wife, to lesser issues, such as how to bake a cake or how often to bathe a baby. These topics and many more were covered in the male-authored books. Most women probably also accepted what male interpreters of the Bible wrote—that they were, by its authority, inferior beings, rightfully subservient to patriarchal rule in family, church, and society. But that, of course, did not stop a woman from wielding whatever influence she could in her day-to-day relationship with father or husband.

Legally, a maiden or a wife was a *femme couverte*, that is, a woman "covered" under the jurisdiction of a father, guardian, or husband. Elizabeth I, once freed from the control of her father the king, was wise enough to stay unmarried. Had she accepted one of the many proposals sent her way, she would have been, throne notwithstanding, theoretically subject to the authority of her husband. A widow escaped, at least temporarily, from this "protection." She had a certain amount of independence and power over her own life. Yet this fact alone disturbed many of the male writers, who exhorted widows to remarry and, always, to rely on the advice of male relatives in choosing a new partner.

Once married, a woman was cautioned, in both writing and training, to love her husband in spite of his faults. Thomas Bentley, who at the end of the sixteenth century published a fat book of prayers for women, wrote a supplication for the woman with a "froward [ornery] and bitter" husband. The solution was for the wife to pray and to "most heartily" thank God for this challenge as well as the opportunity to bear her husband's faults with "more patience, mildness and modesty."[9] Bentley's formidable, three-inch-thick, 1,500-page book included, along with prayers for women, some prayers *by* women, biographies of Biblical women, and dozens of lengthy supplications implicitly acknowledging— as did the "froward husband" prayer—the inferiority of women.

However, not all books belittled women. Females had their supporters among male writers, who praised them and spelled out their finer qualities. Some men wrote in dialogue form, with participants arguing women's virtues and rights as well as limitations.[10] But the dominant sentiment—adopted even by the women speaking in the dialogues—was that a woman's place was in her home, where her good qualities could be appreciated by husband and family. Only in the early seventeenth century—when women became involved in the resurgent controversy over the innate goodness or evil of the female sex—did a handful of pro-female books appear, written by women, to challenge the old views.

A Society of Classes

To be a woman was, at root, to be an imperfect man. Sex was a major defining fact of existence. Gender restrictions, based on male superiority and female subservience, were clear and pervasive. Yet just as important was social class. The kitchenmaid was not the queen; the Puritan was not the prostitute. Customs and laws reinforced class distinctions.

Acceptable apparel for the lady at court was unlawful for a tradesman's daughter to wear. A peasant's everyday labor was forbidden by custom to the yeoman's wife. And education and literacy differed widely, usually by class.

These class and gender hierarchies permeated Early Modern society in England. Philosophers called it "The Great Chain of Being," the precise descending order of all heavenly and earthly beings from God on down. Men and women, kings and commoners—all understood that the peasant's station was below that of his landowner, and in a given social class the woman's was always below the man's.

This book deals with the instructions men gave—in print—to women, the relationships among men, women, and families, and the importance of class restrictions in all relationships.

The audience for these male-authored books was the woman who could read and, through her, the people she supervised in her home. The female reading public came largely from the upper and middle classes. That left many hundreds of thousands of lower-class women who learned their roles through oral instruction, observation of role models, and church teachings. Some learned the rules—or roles—from mistresses for whom they worked. Others, living a hand-to-mouth existence, were less interested in conforming to social rules than they were in earning pennies for survival. Proper behavior was a distinctly secondary matter. As for aristocrats and the wealthy: they could act as they wished because of their position; few could correct or chastise them. So it was the middle class—the lower gentry, tradesmen, yeomen, professionals, and others of a "middling sort"—who were most affected by the prescriptive literature, though members of the upper classes certainly owned and read the books.

The middle class was growing rapidly; it provided an audience that publishers wanted to tap. It was also the group from which most American immigrants derived. In short, the middle class was increasing, not only in influence and power, but in appetite for books.

Female Roles

What *were* the roles of women, and how did women think and feel about their roles? These questions are hard to answer because most women at that time did not feel free to write and publish their own opinions. The past is difficult enough to recover when centuries intervene. Recovering the female past is especially hard because women's lives (with the exception of queens and aristocrats) are underrecorded.

Thus the sizable body of literature concerning women depicts them according to men's views of them. These books by men are our largest source of evidence, if only by default, and provide useful clues to the lives of sixteenth- and seventeenth-century women.

Other sources besides prescriptive literature provide insight into the lives of women. Paintings, artifacts, clothing, and surviving houses are useful. Letters, diaries, handwritten household records, and "receipts" (recipes) by women are valuable (though their numbers are limited, since only literate women had the time and resources to write). Wills, mostly by widows, enumerate personal belongings and private preferences. Court records detail legal decisions pertaining to women. The burgeoning theatre and the lusty humor of the day—expressed in ballads and jest books—provide other (frequently negative) views of female characteristics. And notorious scandals of the time give us insight into the public's moral sensibilities about permissible female behavior.

Still, the most abundant resources are the old printed conduct books, sermons, and instructional guides in which men spelled out for women how to live and behave and handle daily chores. That these instructions came from men did not surprise women of the time; they were accustomed to male directives. Men, in their "naturally" preeminent roles, were the legal heads of households, the preachers, the schoolmasters, the religious and cultural leaders, the instructors. Law, custom, and the church promoted and endorsed male superiority. In such a world, women learned that it was inappropriate for them to speak or act independently in public. "To write for *public*ation" is, by definition, going public. Besides, female writers were at a disadvantage because of their limited education and lack of exposure to the literature of ideas. The women who did write would often apologize for their lack of learning.

To many, real learning and intellect were still locked in the classics, which men could study in grammar schools and universities—places forbidden to women. Under those circumstances it was a rare woman who dared write for publication.

In 1600 London had about 200,000 people; England, perhaps 4 million.[11] Such a largely rural, small population favored conformity. In the preindustrial world most people lived in agricultural households. Neighbors knew neighbors, and one person's personal foibles soon became public knowledge (a living soap opera for a time before television). To flout the norm was to court criticism, or worse. Punishments, such as wearing the scold's bridle, or whippings and dunkings, were embarrassingly public. Conformity, then, was the easier route for women. And plenty of advice on how to conform was available.

Many women lived, as best they could, the way society (and male directives) told them to live. Many who could read would try to emulate the ideals set forth in the books men wrote for them. Women's magazines in the twentieth century offer a corollary. In the 1920s and 1930s these periodicals pictured idyllic family life: cleverly decorated homes, economical but tasteful meals, and beautifully dressed and coiffed women who welcomed their husbands each evening with clean houses and obedient children—women who never missed church on Sunday and read uplifting messages on weekdays. These were wives with enough skill, generosity, beauty, education, and maternal instincts to handle any problems that might arise in the typical "American dream home." The short stories described successful family life, from titillating-but-circumspect teenage stories to happily-ever-after romances. Women looked forward to new issues each month; many readers had several subscriptions. Hundreds of articles answered the needs of the stay-at-home wife and mother. Many, but not all, of these magazines were controlled and edited by men; their articles and short stories, too, were often written by men.[12]

Of course, women who devoured those magazines knew—if they were honest—that they often did not look, act, or feel the way the articles described female life. But the magazines showcased an ideal, a goal that many readers worked hard to reach. Most readers didn't know or care whether the magazines were run by men or women; that awareness came later. Most women of the sixteenth and seventeenth centuries may also have accepted the ideals prescribed for them without questioning the male source.

Clearly, not all women in past or present centuries have behaved according to instructions. In Early Modern England, plays, farces, ribald tales, and antifemale essays ridiculed nonconforming women. In 1615 the popular *Arraignment of Lewde, Idle, Froward, and Unconstant Women,* by Joseph Swetnam, renewed the controversy and spurred a series of publications on the good and evil of the female sex. The humor of the day often depicted women as nagging, disobedient, garrulous, overdressed, oversexed, drunken, and bawdy; of course, that doesn't prove that most women had those characteristics.

In general, respectable or "good" girls and women were expected to stay close to home and learn household skills and duties and little else. They had inferior minds, incapable of handling complex subjects. So said a number of male writers like Billingsley. Many women were forced by circumstance and class to work outside the home, toiling in fields or as servants in someone else's home, or hawking food (or their bodies) in the streets. But they did *not* have access to most professions. Their own occupations were usually tied in some way to domestic work. True, there were a few female professionals and tradespeople: printers (widows who inherited their husband's trade), midwives (though they were beginning to feel competition from increasingly assertive male physicians), and some teachers (by the end of this era). But they were the rare exceptions.

Men's Literature About Women

Men's writing was *prescriptive* and *proscriptive,* but not always *descriptive.* It pictured women according to men's ideals and interpretations. The books prescribe a life different from what women might have described had they been publishing, *and had they been accustomed to assertive roles in an egalitarian society.* Most of the male messages were uniform and repetitive, and when female writers finally produced numerous guidebooks after 1675, many copied the male model. Yet some—those, for example, advocating more education for women—did not. And some men wrote in defense of the female sex or promoted further education for their sisters and wives. They rarely, however, questioned the hierarchy of male over female or the premise that women's roles were primarily domestic.

Most women before 1675 were well aware of the roles set for them by fathers, by husbands, and by male teachers, clerics, and writers. True, girls received domestic and some religious instructions from other females at home, but women in general lacked alternatives to male prescriptions for their place in society. Most, particularly in the growing middle class, simply conformed to the patriarchal authority described in how-to-live books.

It would be easy to presume that this old culture amounts to a quaint and irrelevant anachronism. But much the same situation still exists in many parts of the world. There are societies today where women must cover themselves in a uniformly conservative manner, may not be seen at men's gatherings, are not permitted to drive vehicles, are expected to stay at home most of the time, are discouraged from public activities, cannot vote or hold office, and are subject to severe punishment, even death, for adultery or fornication.

Early Modern male literature reached a wide audience; with rare exceptions, the few books by women did not. In any case, publishers responded to the growing number of women who could read English. Although recent scholarship shows that few women could write, the large number of publications specifically for women indicate that many knew how to read. Between 1475 and 1640 approximately 170 different books in some 500 editions were specifically addressed to females or dealt with subjects of direct concern to women, such as midwifery, household recipes, and how-to-live guides. If each of the 500 editions had a run of 1,000 copies—normal at that time—then 500,000 books for women came onto the market in that 165-year period.[13] These numbers do not include the many general-audience books women were also reading. There was clearly a market for books for women, or publishers would not have produced them in such quantities.

Reading is easier than writing. With enough motivation and a willing tutor it could be learned at home. Writing was a different, more complex skill, historically left to clerics or secretaries; it did not have to be taught in conjunction with reading. Girls learned to read in a number of settings, though much less is known about their education than is recorded about boys. Many studied at home—either their own or another where they were sent to serve and learn. Groups of girls (sometimes orphans) received basic reading and writing instruction, often from visiting male teachers. "Petty" (lower elementary) schools, where girls as well as boys could learn basic English, existed in many villages. A few small, local schools for girls were started, and by the late seventeenth century a number of girls' boarding schools were open, but only for those who could afford them.

Despite their limited opportunities, some women became writers. Often their work was read only by friends, among whom hand-written manuscripts were circulated. They wrote poetry; they translated works from continental and classical languages; they wrote essays (some in response to accusations against their sex); they produced devotional and religious material; they passed down household recipes; they penned letters and journals (and in the case of Margaret Cavendish, Duchess of Newcastle, a full-fledged autobiography). Yet, with the exception of a few books written by mothers for their children, they did not publish conduct or how-to-do-it guides until late in the seventeenth century.

Between 1475, the start of English printing, and 1650, only roughly 125 women are known to have authored printed material of any kind. This is about 1 percent of what was published.[14] Much female writing dealt with religious and devotional minutiae, dull and largely uninformative today. After 1650 the number of female publications increased markedly, but few were instructional guides. The much-maligned Duchess of Newcastle braved criticism of her poetry and creative writing to produce a number of publications in the second half of the seventeenth century, but her work did not venture far into the practical fields of everyday living. On the other hand, Hannah Wolley, with her recipe books, and Jane Sharp, with her midwifery book, *did* publish guidebooks in the third quarter of the seventeenth century. Other women who published guidebooks before 1675 were cautious, mainly providing advice to children on how to live godly and conventional lives and keeping close to the male model. Elizabeth Joceline, whose *Mothers Legacie to Her Unborne Child* was printed posthumously, wrote (speaking of a daughter):

I desire her bringing up may be learning the Bible, as my sisters do, good huswifery, writing and good works. Other learning a woman needs not, though I admire it in those whom God has blest with discretion.[15]

Today the old books by men open a window, if not a door, on sixteenth- and seventeenth-century female life. Recipe books suggest what food and drink women prepared. Medical guides, with instructions for household remedies, reveal the diseases women faced and how they tried to cure them. Prayer books hint at troubles they endured—with or without heavenly intervention. Midwifery books, with their abominable ignorance, disclose disastrous beliefs about conception and birth.

Quotations from these early books are assembled in the chapters that follow. Many will sound bizarre and unbelievable; without some explanation, they are little more than curiosities. The commentary that ties them together is an attempt to give them context and make the lives of women then—and now—more understandable.

Despite the power structure that conferred male dominance over women, the tantalizing fact remains that female rebels existed. Contemporary drama, humor, scandals, and legal cases do more than hint at nonconforming females. They were there—a minority—but in sufficient numbers to keep men busy repeating instructions on the "correct" life, while others wrote scathing works that mocked those who strayed. Class and gender ruled, and male-female equality was far away, but the restrictive life pictured by men for women would one day be challenged by a growing number of female voices who spoke against the patriarchal limits set forth in the books—and times—described here. Despite published cultural restrictions, a few women advised, influenced, or managed the men in their lives.

Today, centuries later, unpublished writing by Tudor-Stuart women is being unearthed; unheralded deeds are receiving more attention; differences in the cultural patterns of the genders are being analyzed. Female history is moving out of the shadow of male lives and deeds, thanks to new discoveries and thinking. But in their own time their voices were whispers among the shouts of the men. ❦

Notes

1. *Bible*, 1 Cor. 11:3.
2. Daniel Rogers, *Matrimonial Honor* (1642), 255.
3. Francis Meres, *Gods Arithmeticke* (1597), D^v.
4. David Cressy, *Literacy and the Social Order: Reading and Writing in Tudor and Stuart England* (Cambridge Univ. Press, 1980), 177.
5. Martin Billingsley, *The Pens Excellencie or the Secretaries Delighte* (1617?), C2^v.
6. Robert Cawdrey, *A Table Alphabeticall . . . gathered for the benefit and helpe of Ladies, Gentlewomen, or any other unskilfull persons* (1604), title page.
7. Roger Thompson, *Women in Stuart England and America* (London and Boston: Routledge & Kegan Paul, 1974), 21–52.
8. See Marcia Guttentag and Paul F. Secord, *Too Many Women? The Sex Ratio Question* (Beverly Hills, London, New Delhi: Sage Publications, 1983) for discussion of male authority in both high and low sex-ratio situations.
9. Thomas Bentley, "The Fifth Lampe of Virginitie" in *The Monument of Matrones* (1582), 73–76.
10. See Robert Vaughan, *A Dialogue Defensyve for Women agaynst Melycyous Detractoures* ([1542]), and Daniel Tuvil, *Asylum Veneris or a Sanctuary for Ladies, justly protecting them, their virtues, and sufficiencies from the foule aspersions and forged imputations of traducing spirits* (1616).
11. Roger Thompson, *Women in Stuart England and America* (London and Boston: Routledge & Kegan Paul, 1974), 32. For population estimates see also E. A. Wrigley and R. S. Schofield, *The Population History of England, 1541–1871* (Cambridge, Mass.: Harvard Univ. Press, 1981).
12. For a good summary of twentieth-century magazines for women see Joanne Meyerowitz, "Beyond the Feminine Mystique: A Re-assessment of Postwar Mass Culture" in *Journal of American History* (Bloomington, Ind.: Organization of American Historians, March 1993), 79, 4:1455–1482.
13. For a detailed discussion of books addressed to women see Suzanne W. Hull, *Chaste, Silent & Obedient, English Books for Women 1475–1640* (San Marino, Calif.: Huntington Publications, 1982, 1988).

14. For a statistical analysis of women's writing in this general period, see Patricia Crawford, "Women's Published Writings 1600–1700" in *Women in English Society 1500–1800*, Mary Prior, ed. (London: Mathuen, 1985), 211–82.
15. Elizabeth Joceline, *The Mothers Legacie to Her Unborne Childe* (1624), B3^{v}.

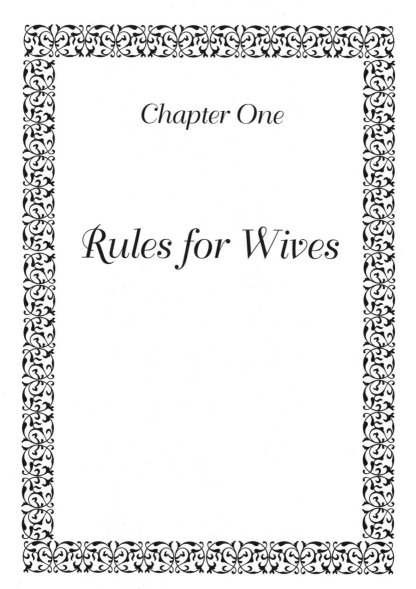

Chapter One

Rules for Wives

The English Gentlewoman

Glory my goale

Grace my guide

Rules for Wives

*L*egally a wife was chattel in sixteenth- and seventeenth-century England. Her person and her property were under the control of her husband. He had the right to rule over her, to dispose of her property, to teach and chastise her, even to beat her.

Before she became a wife, a woman was educated and trained for domestic duties and responsibilities. No matter what social class she belonged to, she had certain skills to learn. Wealthy, aristocratic girls needed more social and management know-how and less of the hands-on practical skills essential, say, to a yeoman's daughter. But each would anticipate the role of wife as her future "job."

For girls of the lower ranks, the choice of a husband could be a personal matter, as titles and major financial stakes were not factors. But matchmaking for upper-class girls was serious business. Although it was the responsibility of the father or guardian to "dispose" of the young women in his family, mothers and grandmothers were often instrumental in finding the proper spouse for a son or daughter. (Some even drew up marriage agreements.) Class, age, religious affiliation, wealth, and compatibility had to be considered in arranging a successful upper-class marriage. Judging by the many anecdotes about unhappy marriages among the aristocracy, compatability may have been more difficult to evaluate than some of the other qualities.

Opposite page:
ENGLISH GENTLEWOMAN, from *The English Gentlewoman*, by Richard Brathwaite (London, 1631). By permission of the Huntington Library, San Marino, Calif.

Once a woman was married, her behavior was spelled out in a vast number of books. There were eulogies and biographies praising good women; ballads and jest books belittled the bad. Sermons and marriage manuals set forth the "proper" roles for each sex. The appropriate position for a woman, regardless of her class, was as a dependent under the tutelage and control of her husband. The law and the church so prescribed.

A summary of laws pertaining to women, called *The Lawes Resolutions of Womens Rights,* was published in England in 1632. The author, identified only by initials, claimed he was writing it as a "peculiar service" to women. It may have been a service, but it was not a popular one. The book was printed only once. Although it is not completely accurate in some of the laws it describes, it does give a vivid picture of the restrictions placed on women's lives and property, as well as the dominance of the husband in marriage. Here is one description of *personal* property laws:

> For thus it is, if before marriage the woman were possessed of horses, meat, sheep, coin, wool, money, plate, and jewels, all manner of movable substance is presently by conjunction [marriage] the husband's, to sell, keep or bequeath if he die. And though he bequeath them not, yet are they the husband's executors and not the wife's which brought them to her husband.[1]

Wives could own—but usually only widows could bequeath—*real* property given to them in premarital agreements or wills. But according to a 1622 book, *Of Domesticall Duties,* the husband still had major control over disposition of that property:

> Now our law saith that every gift, grant or disposition of goods, lands, or other thing whatsoever made by a woman covert . . . if they be done without her husband's consent, are void. For the authority which God hath given an husband, and subjection which he hath laid on a wife, restrain her power and liberty in that which is her own.[2]

The Lawes Resolutions of Womens Rights also confirmed the right of the husband to beat his wife, though the author sympathized with the unfortunate women who received such abuse:

If a man beat an outlaw, a traitor, a pagan, his villein [serf] or his wife
it is dispunishable, because by the law common these persons can have
no action. God send gentlewomen better sport, or better company.[3]

The men who wrote the marriage guides and sermons frequently
cautioned husbands that they must use their authority well and rule their
wives in a gentle, considerate, and benevolent manner. Respect was due
the wife, and husbands were reminded to reprove their wives in private
and to use physical force only after all other methods of control had
failed. But if she was abused or beaten, the wife could expect only
temporary respite from the law:

If it be said that some men are so violent as the wife may be in danger
to have her brains knocked out, and may she not refuse to dwell with
such an one. The answer is she may decline the present brunt [assault],
but she may not forsake the matrimonial society. She may fly to the
magistrate and seek safety with a purpose of returning upon such
security, but she may not fly quite away from him with a purpose of
not returning.[4]

That paragraph and the one that follows were written by William
Whately, an early-seventeenth-century Puritan preacher trained at Cambridge and Oxford. He published a number of devotional tracts, some of
which were highly controversial. His message, below, from *A Bride-Bush,
or a Wedding Sermon,* was that the woman was to stay put, even if it meant
death, because that was where both God and marriage placed her.

For as it is no warrant [defense] for a soldier to quit his standing because
the case falls out so that he must either die or leave it, so neither must
a Christian in any place depart from his place for fear of death, for how
can one spend his life better than in keeping the place where God hath
set him?[5]

Yet there was a double standard. Thomas Bentley expressed the
opinion that the husband should not be so restricted. He wrote, "If she
walk not in thine obedience, cut her off then from thy flesh. Give her a
bill of divorcement and forsake her."[6]

Divorce and marriage dissolutions were possible (witness Henry
VIII), though rare. They were much more obtainable for men than

women—and for the upper classes rather than the rest. Civil divorce required parliamentary approval and thus was available almost exclusively to well-to-do families with contacts in London. Even with such approval, remarriage was usually not an option. The chief ground for divorce—adultery—was based on Biblical teaching. *The Lawes Resolutions of Womens Rights* says:

> The civil law hath many causes of divorce, but by divine and common law, the only sufficient cause is adultery and fornication, which by the canons is carnal and spiritual. The spiritual is heresy and idolatry. They dissolve matrimony for spiritual fornication only where one of the parties is converted to Christian faith and the other, for hatred of his religion, will not cohabit, etc. And this is taken also from St. Paul . . . where he saith, if the unbelieving depart, let him depart.[7]

Most marital advisers, however, avoided the question of divorce. It was easier to talk about responsibilities within a marriage than face the problem of an impossible one. A generation before poet and pamphleteer John Milton penned his well-known essays on divorce, the bold preacher Whately wrote that desertion was grounds for divorce—despite his declaration, quoted above, that women should never desert their marital bed and duties. Elsewhere in the same wedding sermon he declared, "The bond of matrimony is dissolved," and the innocent spouse is "so truly and totally loosed from it, that . . . it shall be no sin for him or her to make a new contract [of marriage] with another person." To church leaders, this was going too far. Whately was forced to apologize to his readers and withdraw this idea in later editions.

Milton's championing of divorce appeared first in 1643. He wrote:

> Indisposition, unfitness or contrariety of mind, arising from a cause in nature unchangeable, hindering and ever likely to hinder the main benefits of conjugal society, which are solace and peace, is a greater reason of divorce than natural frigidity, especially if there be no children, and that there be mutual consent.[8]

Two years later he declared:

> If there be found between the pair a notorious disparity either of wickedness or heresy, the husband by all manner of right is disengaged

from a creature . . . inflicted on him to the vexation of his righteousness. The wife, also, as her subjection is terminated in the Lord, being herself the redeemed of Christ, is not still bound to be the vassal of him who is the bondslave of Satan.[9]

The first quotation from Milton appears to defend divorce in cases of incompatibility, a concept acceptable in modern society but hardly common in the seventeenth century. The second quotation confronts another form of incompatibility that arose when one spouse followed the dictates of the Christian church while the other rejected the faith. These arguments of Milton's for divorce (beyond adultery and desertion) created a furor but had little influence in his lifetime. It would be nearly two centuries before they found their way into civil law and accepted attitudes. Divorce remained unthinkable to many, churchmen and lay-men alike. But the threat of divorce was not all bad, claimed one man in the time of Henry VIII:

> Many things were written in old time in the rebuke of womankind, and divorces sought out, and sharply executed. And now among Christian men those things be sore missed of many, and desired after. For they say their wives would be better, if they knew they might be put away [divorced], except they were gentle.[10]

That paragraph comes from an unlikely source. The writer was Juan Luis Vives, a Roman Catholic adviser to Queen Catherine of Aragon in the raising and education of her daughter, the future Queen Mary Tudor. Like the queen, Vives was a Spaniard. He spent several years in England, but became persona non grata with Henry VIII shortly before Henry shed Catherine and married Anne Boleyn. Meanwhile, Vives wrote *The Instruction of a Christen Woman*, published in Latin in 1523 and translated into English around 1529. His recommendations for female education were conservative but practical. In the short statement quoted above, Vives seems to condone divorce. He is correct that divorces were more easily obtained in the Middle Ages, though it is surprising that he appears to see the threat of divorce as an acceptable stratagem in a Roman Catholic world.

With or without divorce, polygamy was hardly acceptable. Yet Bentley felt it necessary to spell it out in a chapter on "The Duty of Husbands toward their Wives":

> A man ought to be the husband but of one wife. For to have more than one at once is a sign of incontinency, *especially in a bishop or minister.*[Emphasis mine][11]

In the sixteenth century the increasingly literate middle class turned to a growing quantity of printed materials for guidance in everyday living. Answers to matrimonial questions—plus detailed descriptions of the ideal husband and wife—were found in marriage manuals, printed wedding sermons, household instruction books, and social or philosophical essays. Although they were not only for women (both sexes wanted to know their specific roles and duties in marriage), many had chapters addressed to women and wives, with precise instructions on proper behavior. Women were warned to walk with eyes down; to avoid idleness, suspicious company, and unsuitable clothing; to stay at home; and to acknowledge their own inferiority. Obedience and a sense of subservience were requirements repeated over and over. This quotation on "the woman's great and chief commandment" is typical:

> The man (we know) was first created, as a perfect creature, and not the woman with him at the same instant, as we know both sexes of all other creatures were contemporary. Not so here. But, after his constitution and frame ended, then was she thought of. Secondly, she was not made of the same matter with the man equally, but she was made and framed of the man by a rib taken from the man. And thirdly, she was made for the man's use and benefit as a meet helper.[12]

Authority for male domination came from Saint Paul's statement in 1 Corinthians 11, while the Biblical story of Adam and Eve (man created by God; woman created later from man's rib to be his helper) was further "proof."

Edmund Tilney argued in 1568 that religious laws were not the only ones supporting male supremacy:

> For indeed both divine and human laws in our religion giveth the man absolute authority over the woman in all places. And . . . reason doth

confirm the same, the man [having] not only skill and experience to be required but also capacity to comprehend, wisdom to understand, strength to execute, solicitude to prosecute, patience to suffer, means to sustain, and above all a great courage to accomplish, all which are commonly in a man, but in a woman very rare.[13]

Tilney wielded considerable power, as he was Master of Revels at the English Court for over thirty years and, for most of that time, was also the censor of all plays. His was an old, aristocratic family. *The Flower of Friendshippe*, from which the above quotation is taken, is a form of "courtesy book" mimicking the style and some of the content of the earlier *Courtyer* by the Italian writer Baldassare Castiglione.

Such perfection as he describes here must have been a marvel to see. Tilney's views, like Billingsley's, presupposed inadequacies—physiological inferiority—in the female brain.

Not everything written on the differences between the sexes was solemn and prescriptive, however. After all, it was an age of poetry and ballads. Women who were unlikely to read sermons could get the message in popular rhymes:

Now when thou art become a wife,
And hast an husband to thy mind,
See thou provoke him not to strife,
Lest haply he do prove unkind.
Acknowledge that he is thine head,
And hath of thee the governance,
And that thou must of him be led,
According to God's ordinance.[14]

Or:

Obedience first, thy will to his must fit,
(He is the pilot that must govern it).
It man condemns of inability,
When women rule that is born to obey.[15]

Whately put salt in the wound by insisting that:

The wife's special duty may fitly be referred to two heads. First, she must acknowledge her inferiority. Secondly, she must carry herself as

37

an inferior. First then, every good woman must suffer herself to be convinced in judgment that she is not her husband's equal (yea, that her husband is her better by far) without which it is not possible there should be any contentment, either in her heart or in her house. Where the woman stands upon terms of equality with her husband (much more if she will needs account herself his better) the very root of all good carriage is quite withered. . . . Whosoever therefore doth desire or purpose to be a good wife, or to live comfortably, let her set down this conclusion within her soul: mine husband is my superior, my better; he hath authority and rule over me. Nature hath given it him.[16]

There was no question of equality between the sexes on earth, though Francis Meres, an ordained priest and scholar, holding out a carrot, said:

Therefore love your husbands here, and if they reward it not, it shall be rewarded in Heaven. Be obedient to them here, and ye shall be made equal with them in Heaven. Be humble and lowly here, and ye shall be exalted in Heaven. Be clothed with modesty here, and ye shall be clothed with honor in Heaven.[17]

Tilney went so far as to write that barbarian men and women might believe in equality, but never Christians.[18]

A thorny problem arose when a woman felt her husband was ordering her to act against the word of God. Milton said, "A right believer ought to divorce an idolatrous heretic,"[19] but other writers had a hard time supporting independent action by a wife without her husband's approval. The wife was advised to try gentle persuasion or call in other male members of the family or parish to change her husband's mind, rather than defy his order. As Whately put it in his 1617 book:

In whatsoever matter a woman's yielding to her husband shall not prove a rebellion against her maker, in that matter she is bound in conscience to yield unto him without any further question.[20]

Underlying all relationships, the basic assumption continued to be a belief in the natural superiority of the male sex. This included not only the obvious physical prowess of men but their presumed mental acuity as well. It was hard for most writers to accept that a woman might have a sharper mind or be the wiser partner in a marriage. Milton, a liberal for his day, was at least willing to tackle the problem, though his analysis was confusing. On the one hand, he said:

> Not but that particular exceptions may have place, if she exceed her husband in prudence and dexterity, and he contentedly yield, for then a superior and more natural law comes in, that the wiser should govern the less wise, whether male or female.[21]

But even Milton waffled. He could not accept that a man should "contentedly yield" to a woman's strength and leadership; he reverted to the Biblical admonition that woman was made to be a helpmate. In the next quotation he seems to say that a wife must be subservient, regardless of her intelligence, and the husband must never abdicate his "birthright" of superiority to a woman who might flaunt her wisdom or use it to control the man:

> . . . seeing woman was purposely made for man, and he her head, it cannot stand before the breath of this divine utterance that man, the portraiture of God, joining to himself for his intended good and solace, an inferior sex, should so become her thrall [servant] whose willfulness or inability to be a wife frustrates the occasional end of her creation, but that he may acquit himself to freedom by his natural birthright, and that indelible character of priority which God crowned him with.[22]

There was also the problem—in a country so dominated by class structure—of what to do when the wife was superior by birth or wealth. Whately faced this issue but again concluded that the husband's natural preeminence supersedes all other conditions:

> I am (thinketh some woman) of as good birth and parts as himself, perhaps better. My wealth, wit, parentage, before I met with him, did equal or surpass him. And why should I count myself his inferior to whom I am no way inferior in gifts or sufficiencies?. . . Let us grant for the time that in gifts thou art his better, . . . yet understand for answer that so may thy servant exceed thee as much as thou dost him . . . yet loath would the wife be (I think) that the servant should deny both her husband and herself the name of betters. Know then that man may be superior in place and power to one to whom he is inferior in gifts and sufficiencies, and therefore know also that thou dost wickedly abuse

the good parts that God hath given in seeking thence to infringe thine husband's superiority over thee.[23]

Here again, the natural hierarchy—the "Great Chain of Being" placing the master above the servant, the man above the woman, the parent above the child—supersedes all other qualities. Every woman, then, must concede that her husband is her "better" no matter what qualities she brings to the marriage.

> True it is that some women are wiser and more discreet than their husbands . . . yet still a great part of the discretion of such women shall rest in acknowledging their husbands to be their heads and so using the graces that they have received of the Lord that their husbands may be honored, not condemned.[24]

The clever woman, according to this next quotation, is one who uses her own personal talents to promote those of her "better" husband. It is the old principle of the power behind the throne. That power must be subtle, allowing all glory to devolve on the husband. The woman's role was seen as a supportive one—to the point of crediting her husband with wisdom she discreetly imparted to him. Vives wrote:

> The woman is not reckoned the more worshipful among men that presumeth to have mastery above her husband, but the more foolish and the more worthy to be mocked. Yea, and more over than that, cursed and unhappy, the which turneth backward the laws of nature like as though a soldier would rule his captain or the moon would stand above the sun, or the arm above the head. For in wedlock, the man resembleth the reason, and the woman the body. Now reason ought to rule, and the body to obey, if a man will live. Also St. Paul sayeth, "The head of the woman is the man."[25]

The notion of man's superiority affected all people, from the queens on down. Queen Elizabeth was well aware that social and legal constraints could harness her if she had a consort. So she toyed with suitors, but remained single. Queens were not the only women to find the marital *status quo* objectionable, else why so many male discourses on a wife's inferiority and the need to submit to her husband's will? And why was there so much male humor at the expense of nonconforming and otherwise "perverse" wives? Women—thought men—needed constant prodding to toe the line. If sober sermons did not work, there were always jests and facetious barbs to press home the point. Elizabethan England thrived on rhymes that ridiculed women and scorned the man who let a woman rule him:

> Yet, I will ever bear my father's mind
> I scorn as much to stoop to women kind
> For if I should, then all men would me hate
> Because from manhood I degenerate
> And surely I should have the love of no man
> If I were such a slave unto a woman
> Which to prevent, or to avoid ill speeches
> I'll look that thou shalt never wear the breeches.[26]

Song writers, poets, and hack writers made money and reputations by poking fun at shrews and scolds, nagging wives and village gossips. Shakespeare's Kate in *The Taming of the Shrew* made good theatre, but she was expected to learn the error of her ways by the end of the last act. There was also a wealth of one-liners at the expense of wives, good or bad. Here are two:

> Four things kill a man before his time: a sad or sorrowful family, meat or drink immoderately taken, a pestilent air, and a fair wife.[27]

And:

> Those men grow soon rich whose bees prosper and their wives perish, or whose sheep and oxen thrive with them, and their wives fail them.[28]

The inferences here are that a fair wife would stray or be lured away, and a man would be wealthier without a spendthrift wife.

Besides the cuckolding and spendthrift wives, a favorite target of male humor was the talkative or clever wife. The author of this rhyme, Archibald Armstrong, was jester to the court of James I and author of a jestbook called *A Banquet of Jests*:

> A woman lately fiercely did assail
> Her husband with sharp tongue but sharper nail.
> But one that heard and saw it, to her said,

41

Why do you use him thus, he is your head.
He is my head indeed, says she, 'tis true.
Sir, I may scratch my head, and so may you.[29]

Another facetious tale was written by the prolific Richard Brathwaite, who wrote in many genres using a number of pseudonyms. In his *Ar't Asleep Husband?*, a book of "witty jests, merry tales, and other pleasant passages," a shrew is pictured on the frontispiece, pestering her husband with chatter in bed. The caption reads:

This wife a wondrous racket means to keep,
While th'husband seems to sleep but does not sleep:
But she might full as well her lecture smother,
For entering one ear, it goes out at t'other.[30]

Armstrong, the jester, claimed even the grave couldn't silence some wives:

Here lies a woman no man can deny it.
She rests in peace, although she lived unquiet.
Her husband prays, if by her grave you walk,
You'll gently tread, for if she wakes she'll talk.[31]

In a more serious vein, a book with the patronizing title *Counsel to the Husband: To the Wife Instruction* warned wives that:

To fall out, to brawl, to lour [frown], to be sullen and fret, or (which is a degree worse) . . . to scold and speak presumpuously, this is beyond her place. It is intolerable contention.[32]

A strange and rather barbaric punishment could be meted out to the shrew or scold (both were terms used for talkative or chiding women). An iron device called the "branks" or a "scold's bridle" was placed over her head. It had a tongue depressor that prevented talking. The woman would then be paraded through the streets or placed on public display. (See the illustration on the cover.)

John Taylor, famous as the Water Poet in the 1640s, published an early needlework guide in which he cautioned women to remain silent. *The Needles Excellency*, in a brief introduction called "The Praise of the Needle," makes this jab at garrulous women:

And for my country's quiet, I should like,
That womenkind should use no other pike,
It will increase their peace, enlarge their store,
To use their tongues less and their needles more,
The needle's sharpness profit yields, and pleasure,
But sharpness of the tongue bites out of measure.[33]

And the conservative Vives, in a somber note, warned wives not
to nag:

There is nothing that so soon casteth the mind of the husband from his
wife as doth much scolding and chiding and her mischievous tongue,
which Solomon likeneth unto a dropping and raining house roof in the
winter, because that both driveth the man forth at the door.[34]

The husband might be "driven forth at the door," but the woman
was expected to stay indoors and not go "abroad." A woman's place was
in the home, and the only reasons for going out were:

First, to come to holy meetings, according to the duty of Godliness. The
second, to visit such as stand in need, as the duty of love and charity
do require. The third, for employment and provision in household
affairs committed to her charge. And lastly, with her husband when he
shall require.[35]

If she could not go out into the greater world, a woman could expect
to manage her own house. Most men conceded rule of the house and
servants to their wives—subject, of course, to the man's overall jurisdiction. The argument, according to Whately, was that the husband should
not have to bother with the "small business of the family," but rather

he should permit his wife to rule under him and give her leave to know
more than himself who hath weightier matters and more nearly touching the welfare of his household to exercise his knowledge in.[36]

Another author, Patrick Hannay, wrote in his *Happy Husband:*

As it befits not man for to embrace
Domestic charge, so it's not woman's place
For to be busied with affairs abroad.
For that weak sex, it is too great a load,

And it's unseemly, and doth both disgrace,
When either doth usurp the other's place.[37]

It was the husband's duty to delegate authority within the household.
He could deputize the wife in his absence (including lengthy, enforced
absences during the Civil War) and leave the everyday activities in the
house under her control, but he could never abdicate overall power:

> The man must divide the offices and affairs of the house with his wife,
> giving her authority over all things in his absence, and his presence
> also, over household matters and such things as are more proper and
> agreeable to that sex, causing her to be feared, reverenced and obeyed
> of the children, men-servants and maidservants, as himself.

This is from Peter de la Primaudaye's *French Academie*. Popular
enough to go into five editions, this late-sixteenth-century work asserted
that the man always had the final say:

> As if one take two sounds that agree well, the *bass* [emphasis mine] is
> always more heard, so in a well-ruled and ordered house, all things are
> done by the consent of both parties, but yet so that it is always apparent
> that things are done by the direction, counsel and invention of the
> husband.[38]

The musical metaphor turned up in another book, but this time the
husband becomes, not the bass voice, but the "strongest and highest":

> When in a lute or other musical instrument, two strings concurring in
> one tune, the sound nevertheless is imputed to the *strongest and highest*
> [emphasis mine], so in a well-ordered household there must be a
> communication and consent of counsel and will between the husband
> and the wife, yet such as the counsel and commandment may rest in
> the husband.[39]

The dos and don'ts for wives were many and arduous. If a woman
felt discouraged or needed support, she could always turn to prayer. In
fact, she had hundreds of prayers to choose from, including the one by
Bentley cited in this book's Introduction for the wife with a "froward"
husband. If stuck with such a mate, she was to pray:

O most wise and provident God which in the beginning didst create man in thine own image, and out of him didst make the woman, and didst bring her unto the man, that she might be an helper unto him. . . . I beseech thee to make him an head unto me, and myself an helper unto him, according to my creation . . . and if it be thy good pleasure with frowardness, bitterness and unkindness, yea the hatred and disdain of my husband, thus to correct me for my fault, I most heartily thank thee for it.[40]

Presumably, not all husbands were lovable, but wives were to love them regardless. Men, though, were admittedly less loyal. La Primaudaye hardly endeared himself to wives when he allowed that his sex was inferior in at least one characteristic:

Histories are plentiful in showing the great love of women towards their husbands. Yea, I will not be afraid to speak it, men are far inferior unto them in perfection of love.[41]

In fact, men expected superior treatment from women:

Let her also by sweet words and loving deeds show unto him all the signs of affection she can, considering that some husbands, having been accustomed to the amorous courtesies of other women, will think that their wives set no great store by them if they show them not the like or greater.[42]

Wives were not only to love their husbands but also to close their eyes to any shortcomings, or so said William Gouge in his *Of Domesticall Duties*:

Wives ought in regard of their husbands to surmise no evil whereof they have not sure proof and evidence, but rather interpret everything in better part and follow the rule of love which beareth all things, believeth all things, hopeth all things, endureth all things. If they note any defects of nature and deformity of body or any enormous and notorious vices in their husband, then ought they to turn their eyes and thoughts from his person to his place and from his vicious qualities to his honorable office (which is to be an husband), and this will abate that vile esteem which otherwise might be occasioned from the forenamed means.[43]

In other words, what was forgivable in a husband was not acceptable in a wife, whose faults or vices would be handled differently:

> Now if the husband chance to espy any fault in his wife, either in words, gesture, or doings, he must reprehend her, not reproachfully nor angerly, but as one that is careful of her honesty and what opinion others carry of her, and this must always be done secretly between themselves, remembering the saying that a man must neither chide nor play with his wife in the presence of others, for the one betrayeth her imperfections, and the other his folly.[44]

The common rules for housewives were written by another popular and prolific seventeenth-century author, Gervase Markham. He summarized them as follows:

> Our English housewife must be of chaste thought, stout courage, patient, untired, watchful, diligent, witty, pleasant, constant in friendship, full of good neighborhood, wise in discourse, but not frequent therein, sharp and quick of speech, but not bitter or talkative, secret in her affairs, comfortable in her counsels, and generally skillful in the worthy knowledges which do belong to her vocation.[45]

Add to this La Primaudaye's standard rules for subservient behavior, "Wives must be modest, wise, chaste, keepers at home, lovers of their husbands, and subject unto them,"[46] and the restrictions are quite clear.

To be fair to the male writers, there were those who touted women's admirable qualities. The more popular, multiedition books, however, were the more antifemale, but all was not vitriolic or based on assumptions of female inferiority. Daniel Tuvil's *Asylum Veneris* was divided into ten sections detailing women's worth. Tuvil wrote of their beauty, chastity, outward modesty, humility, silence, constant affections, learning and knowledge, wisdom, discretion, valour, and courage.[47] He claimed:

> Learning in the breast of a woman is likened by their stoical adversaries to a sword in the hands of a madman. . . . Learning, we see, is an ornament and a decency most expedient for women, were it for no other respect than to supply, as occasion may require, the defects that are in men.[48]

But it is hard to find anyone in English print, including Tuvil, who believed women should be placed in positions of superiority to men. They were, instead, to be encouraged to stay and do a good job with their distaff duties, but without competing for male prerogatives. After all, men needed to be waited on, and women were the ones to do it.

There were men who apologized, in a limited and patronizing manner, for any offense they might have caused in humbling women. A sermon preached at an aristocratic wedding, and published in 1607, included this justification:

> Ladies and Gentlewomen, I beseech you mistake me not, and impute no partiality to me. If I have said anything sharply, yet know that I have said nothing against the good, but all against evil women, yea nothing against the sex, but all against the sins of women.[49]

It continues, comparing the ranking of men and women to that of parents and children. Orders are given by parents to children; similarly, orders are given by husbands to wives, on the assumption that men are the stronger and that they naturally carry greater burdens and knowledge.

With all these rules, chores, and perils hanging over their heads, why were women so eager to find husbands? One compelling reason was economic. Few women made or inherited enough money to support themselves adequately. What is more, it was a buyer's market for women and wives. Overall, women outnumbered men. More females than males survived the perils of childhood, disease, accidents, and war, despite the dangers of childbirth.

A woman was taught that her main job in life was to be a housewife, to produce the next generation, and to work with and for her husband. There were few good alternatives if she wanted to eat and have a roof over her head. Given these conditions, a woman might well be apprehensive, judging by this wise advice:

> Ye widows and maidens who are free, be not too free and forward in giving your consent [in marriage] to whom you know not. Among other motives, oft think of this point of subjection to which all wives are bound. . . . After you are married it is in vain to think of freedom from

subjection. By taking husbands and giving yourselves to be wives, you bind yourselves to the bow of the man, as long as he liveth.[50]

Sometimes the rules as set forth in books had the anticipated results, namely, obedient and subservient wives and daughters. Sometimes they did not. There are famous examples in fiction and real life to illustrate both.

First, there were the "good" women like Katherine Stubbes. One of the most popular of all books in this period was one, by Philip Stubbes, that described the life and death of his young wife Katherine. An avid antipapist Puritan, she is said to have sought her husband's guidance in all matters, particularly religious, and to have been a constant reader of the Bible and other solemn religious texts. Death during childbirth at age eighteen did not diminish her virtue: she was described as fearless and joyful at the prospect of entering into everlasting life with Christ.

By contrast, strong, successful, and independent wives existed, though their successes were usually achieved through association with husbands or lovers. For example, there were women printers who successfully inherited their husband's businesses. And there was Elizabeth Hardwick Talbot, Countess of Shrewsbury, better known as Bess of Hardwick, who parlayed four marriages with wealthy men into a personal fortune, which she used to create important country estates and a place in the highest ranks of the aristocracy for her heirs. She may have behaved outwardly in a demure manner that pleased her husbands, while in fact she became an active, independent lady of considerable power, talent, and influence.

Both submission and assertion can be seen in the letters of Arbella Stuart, granddaughter of Bess of Hardwick and, at one time, considered the possible heiress to the English throne. Submissive in her dealings with King James I, in other letters she nonetheless shows an obviously independent spirit. She lived a short and frustrated life in which neither subservience nor an attempt at independence gave her a satisfactory situation.

Literature provides tales of other women. There are examples in Shakespeare's plays: the rebellious Kate (in *The Taming of the Shrew*) and the playfully strong Beatrice (in *Much Ado About Nothing*), for two. The best example of the conforming woman is Patient Griselda, whose story comes down from Bocaccio's *Decameron* and from Chaucer's "Clerk's Tale." Well known to Early Modern readers, Griselda's subservience and quiet patience remain constant even when her husband puts her through unbelievable trials to prove her faithful love and virtue. She is an extreme example of the obedient, uncomplaining wife.

One of Griselda's opposites is the Wife of Bath. The Wife, one of Chaucer's pilgrims, survives five husbands and attains a certain independence and self-reliance in the course of all those widowhoods. She is an earthy character whose tale during the trip to Canterbury suggests that what women want most is sovereignty or power, thus usurping the normal prerogative of men. Her story is one of rebellion against the fixed idea of male dominance.

Meek, deeply religious, obedient wives as well as boisterous, independent, and strong women can be found in both the factual accounts and the fiction of the time. Although laws supported the concept of women as chattel, the lives of individual women suggest that they were not always treated as such. Some women, like the Lady Arbella, tried to be either meek or bold, depending on circumstances. But the written directives for wives clearly promoted the meeker alternative. Wives were to be helpmates to their husbands and accept their domination. They were to be Katherines, not Besses. ❦

Notes

1. T. E., *The Lawes Resolutions of Womens Rights* (1632), 130.
2. William Gouge, *Of Domesticall Duties* (1622), 296, 298.
3. T. E., 128.
4. William Whately, *A Bride-Bush, or a Wedding Sermon* (1619), 214.
5. Ibid.
6. Thomas Bentley, *The Monument of Matrones* (1582), "Sixth Lamp," 21.
7. T. E., 65.
8. John Milton, "The Doctrine and Discipline of Divorce" (1643), pp. 217–356.
9. Milton, *Tetrachordon* (1645), 4–5. Reprint in *Complete Prose Works of John Milton*, pp. 571–718.
10. Juan Luis Vives, *The Instruction of a Christen Woman* (1541), 82^v.
11. Bentley, 12.
12. Daniel Rogers, *Matrimonial Honor* (1642), 253–55.
13. Edmund Tilney, *The Flower of Friendshippe* (1568), E1.
14. Robert Crowley, *The Voyce of the Laste Trumpet* (1549), Diiii.
15. Patrick Hannay, *A Happy Husband* (1619), C1.
16. Whately, 189.
17. Francis Meres, *Gods Arithmeticke* (1597), D1^v.
18. Tilney, E1.
19. Milton, "The Doctrine and Discipline of Divorce" in *Complete Prose Works of John Milton* (Yale Univ. Press, 1959), Vol.II, 264–65.
20. Whately, 206.
21. Milton, *Tetrachordon*, 3.
22. Ibid.
23. Whately, 191.
24. Robert Cleaver, *A Codly [Godly] Form of Household Governement* (1598), 226.
25. Vives, 71^{v,} 72.
26. Humfrey Crouch, "Love's Court of Conscience" (1637) in J. Payne Collier, ed., *Illustrations of Old English Literature* (1866), 16.
27. Thomas Heywood, *A Curtaine Lecture* (1637), 148.
28. Ibid, 149.
29. Archibald Armstrong, *A Banquet of Jests* (1639), 77.

30. Richard Brathwaite, *Ar't Asleepe Husband? A Boulster Lecture* (1640), frontis. Brathwaite is best known for his oft-quoted conduct books, *The English Gentlewoman* and *The English Gentleman*.

31. Armstrong, 78.

32. Ste. B., *Counsel to the Husband; To the Wife Instruction* (1608), 62.

33. John Taylor, *The Needles Excellency* (1631), A, A^v.

34. Vives, 82^v.

35. Cleaver, 229–30.

36. Whately, 148–49 [150].

37. Hannay, C3^v.

38. Peter de la Primaudaye, *The French Academie* (1586), 508.

39. Cleaver, 225.

40. Bentley, "Fifth Lamp," 73–75.

41. La Primaudaye, 522.

42. *The Court of Good Counsell* (1607), D4^v.

43. Gouge, 276–77.

44. *The Court of Good Counsell*, C4^v.

45. Gervase Markham, *The English House-wife* (1631), 4.

46. La Primaudaye, 512.

47. Daniel Tuvil, *Asylum Veneris or a Sanctuary for Ladies* (1616), "Contents."

48. Ibid., 87.

49. Robert Wilkinson, *The Merchant Royall* (1607), 34–35.

50. Gouge, 340.

Chapter Two

Health Habits
and
Household
Remedies

Health Habits
and Household Remedies

*D*ependable information on medicine and the human body was sadly lacking in the sixteenth and seventeenth centuries. Magic, quackery, astrology, and unreliable classical theories filled the void. Several kinds of medical practitioners made a living selling cures or offering their services as experts.

Those men who had university educations, often studying medicine in Italy and France, claimed to be the "professional" physicians. Their training was based on classical texts, in the original Greek and Latin, by Hippocrates, Aristotle, Galen, and others. These physicians learned to treat ailments by balancing the so-called "four humors" (black bile, yellow bile, phlegm, and blood) in each patient. This odd approach was derived from the ancient Greeks and died out only in the nineteenth century. In its various forms, the theory of the four humors dealt with mental and emotional stimuli, control of body temperature, and skin dampness or dryness, as well as diet, elimination, sleep, and exercise. The physicians' knowledge was locked up in languages unfamiliar to most of the population, so doctors could claim they had special secrets for curing the sick. Because they hewed to the ancient theories, physicians did not generally use a hands-on, empirical approach. And they were not above magic, astrology, or remedies made of weird ingredients.

Until the sixteenth century, physicians were drawn from the ranks of priests, monks, and other ecclesiastics. But as humanistic thought spread after the Reformation, medical practice became separated from the church and the new kind of lay physician emerged. Unfortunately, the doctors' major achievement in the sixteenth and seventeenth centuries was not in advancing medical knowledge but rather in organizing themselves into a professional association to keep out those whom they found unsuitable. The unqualified included barbers, surgeons, apothecaries, midwives, housewives, "wise women," and others who were now lumped under the category of quacks.

The new organization was the Royal College of Physicians, established in 1518 with the blessing of King Henry VIII. It was an attempt to license medical practitioners and control access to, and dissemination of, medical information. Under terms of the College, the church retained much control over the medical profession, since licenses to practice medicine were issued by bishops. But the chief complaint of the professional physicians was that unlicensed and "unqualified" persons continued to intrude on their territory. College-licensed doctors considered themselves superior not only to uneducated healers—most of whom were women—but also to barbers, surgeons, and apothecaries, who were wont to offer medical advice on the side.

The barbers and surgeons gradually combined and organized; they took over the setting of broken bones and the bleeding of patients. Apothecaries were the druggists; the cures they dispensed were made of everything from herbs to minerals and metals. "But," claims a modern-day medical historian:

> The apothecary was still a variety of grocer, the surgeon still a variety
> of barber, and the physician but just ceasing to be an ecclesiastic.[1]

"Trained" physicians were exclusively men. Their educational opportunities were not available to women. As physicians tried to consolidate their control over the medical profession, they came into conflict, not only with the apothecaries and surgeons, but also with female care-givers—the midwives, "wise women," and wives who considered the physical care of their families and retainers to be part of a housewife's duties.

With the introduction of printing in England around 1475 and the growing number of women who could read, literate housewives became a market for medical information. The men who wrote or compiled the guidebooks rounded up all kinds of hints and recipes under titles like *A Delightful Daily Exercise for Ladies and Gentlewomen; A Closet for Ladies and Gentlewomen; The English House-wife; The Charitable Physitian;* and *The Treasury of Hidden Secrets, Commonly Called the Good-Huswives Closet of Provision for the Health of Her Houshold*. The title page of this last book said it was

> Gathered out of sundry experiments lately practiced by men of great knowledge, and now newly enlarged with divers necessary physic helps and knowledge of the names and disposition of diseases that most commonly happen to men and women. Not impertinent for every good housewife to use in her house, amongst her own family.

Some of the guidebooks concentrated on "Physic and Chirurgery" (medical science and surgery). Others had recipes ranging from food and drinks to bug killers along with cures for every kind of physical problem. (*The Widowes Treasure* even included "Many profitable and wholesome medicines for sundry diseases in cattle.") Women sought such information, for they were still preparing the remedies for everything from corns to the plague, and their duties extended from assisting at childbirth to embalming the dead.

A wife in Early Modern England performed many duties, including preparation of many more homemade items than people make today. She was in charge of housekeeping (cooking, cleaning, laundry), child care, brewing, distilling, cheese and butter making, care of barnyard animals, clothes making, kitchen gardening, and (in well-to-do, middle-class families) the supervision and training of a staff of workers. Not the least of her duties were the concoction and stocking of remedies for accidents and illness.

Women had a long history as midwives and healers, but the new male doctors poured scorn on those efforts and tried to keep medical knowledge for themselves. At the same time, other men—sometimes compilers or hack writers—willingly published medical "secrets," midwifery books, and household remedies. They also began to advertise their wares and services in print. Few, if any, of the remedy books were by licensed English doctors. Protective of their newly organized profession, physicians were loath to make public their medical knowledge or sign their names to household guidebooks. Several of the books, however, were translations of medical guides by foreign doctors. Half a dozen are by unknown authors (possibly doctors or even women). Most likely they were male compilers like Gervase Markham, a popular early hack writer of guidebooks for women, but not a doctor. He claimed in his *English Huswife* that it "was an approved manuscript . . . belonging sometime to an honorable personage of this kingdom who was a singular amongst those of her rank. . . ." He claimed he was merely organizing her material for publication. *The Ladies Cabinet Opened* (published in 1639 by an unknown writer), *The Ladies Cabinet Enlarged and Opened* (a 1654 publication by "M. B." but similar to the 1639 book), and *The Queens Closet Opened* (purportedly from the records of King Charles I's wife, Queen Henrietta Maria) all claimed to be collections of remedies from the records of royal or aristocratic women. *The Queens Closet Opened* even lists members of the royal family, several prominent noble ladies, a number of doctors, and a few "chirurgians" (surgeons) as "prescribers and approvers" of individual remedies.

The medical quotations in this chapter come from some two dozen of these books. It is this body of laymen's literature, along with women's own experience and word-of-mouth training, that allowed female midwives, healers, and housewives to continue their traditional healing roles despite attempts by professional physicians to take over their work.

So there were conflicting messages: yes, a woman was capable of being a healer or midwife, and there were books of cures and preventives to help her; and no, women were not competent, and their families should rely only on the professionals. Sadly, the pregnant, sick, and maimed often didn't win either way. The basic knowledge just wasn't available. But female healers and midwives at least had the advantage of experience, not merely book learning. Also, the services of professional physicians were expensive, so common folk continued to rely on local wise women or healers, apothecaries, surgeons, and, not least, on the housewife with a good knowledge of homemade medications. Although this era marked the beginning of male domination of the medical world, kitchen medicine still had a prominent place.

Remedies and recipes may have come from women, as some of the male authors claimed, but none were published openly as such until the second half of the seventeenth century. A number of manuscripts— hand-written guides belonging to individual women or families—survive from the earlier period, but almost none were printed at that time. Exceptions include the few pages published in 1622 by Elizabeth Clinton, Countess of Lincoln—a work devoted entirely to her belief that women should nurse their own babies—and Sarah Jinner's tiny, short- lived *Almanac* of the late 1650s, which included—along with the usual astrological data—a few cures for female ailments (for example, "Pills to expel a dead child"). Neither was a book of general remedies. In 1653, two popular books, *A Choice Manual or Rare and Select Secrets in Physics and Chyrurgery* and *A True Gentlewomans Delight* (reputedly by the Countess of Kent), were published posthumously. The first of Hannah Wolley's practical guidebooks came on the market in the next decade. In the 1670s there were more Wolley books and the first major midwifery book by an Englishwoman, Jane Sharp. Women were getting into the how-to-do-it business, but most medical collections continued to be produced by men.

Yet women healers still had a number of male supporters. Soon after the founding of the Royal College of Physicians, Juan Luis Vives defended housewives in their roles as healers and medicine makers. In fact, he came close to endorsing the old proverb, "Kitchen physic is the best physic":

> Because the business and charge within the house lyeth upon the woman's hand, I would she should know medicines and salves for such diseases as be common, and reign almost daily, and have those medi- cines ever prepared ready in some closet wherewith she may help her husband, her little children, and her household meny [menial], when any needeth, that she need not oft to send for the physician, or buy all thing[s] of the apothecary.[2]

But Vives was not a doctor, and doctors felt increasingly that the fine art of "physic" was their bailiwick, far beyond the ken of the most skillful women. Yet they could not prevent all professional advice, particularly translations of foreign medical books, from reaching housewives. The work of a French physician, Philibert Guibert (translated into English in 1639), begins:

> I have written familiarly in this little book the manner to make and prepare in the house these remedies which are practised daily by the best and faithfulest physicians against all sorts of diseases, the which you may easily make yourself.[3]

Despite the strictures of the medical profession, Guibert's work promised that any good physician would help if the housewife had trouble concocting the remedies.

The most prolific and popular of the Englishmen writing medical guidebooks in the second half of the seventeenth century was Nicholas Culpeper. He practiced as a doctor and called himself a physician but apparently had little or no university training. He aroused the wrath of the medical profession by translating one of their secret, classical texts and by writing practical medical guides, such as *A Directory for Midwives*. New books attributed to Culpeper (possibly assembled by his widow) continued to appear long after his death in 1654.

Looking at the Books of Remedies

What did housewives find in the guidebooks? Some contained age-old remedies; some spelled out recipes for medicines that women as well as apothecaries might make; several long books discoursed on how to become pregnant (see the chapter "Misconceptions on Conception" in this book), with small appendices on the care of the newborn; and some offered several cures for the same problem (you could take your choice). All assumed their readers were familiar with the art of distilling water and with the dozens of herbs, pharmaceuticals, metals, and minerals involved in the remedies.

Household remedies depended largely on herbs, flowers, fruits, and roots as well as animal ingredients easily found in rural England. Some of the plant materials are still common today. Others, less common, are defined in the *Oxford English Dictionary* as "formerly much cultivated for medicinal purposes." Herbal remedies ranged from "simples"—medicines of only one ingredient, normally a plant or herb considered a specific remedy for the problem—to complicated cures using many herbs and other ingredients.

According to the Guibert book, drugs and herbs could be bought from druggists or "the herborists or herb women" if the housewife could not provide them herself, and for

> those which live in the country, the physicians of that place will give them acknowledgement of the said simples, and for the medicaments compounded, he will certify you where you shall have them reasonable and faithfully composed.[4]

Guibert assumes a friendly relationship between housewives and local doctors, and this may well have been the norm, particularly in rural England. His book listed dozens of "medicaments simple," with their prices at the apothecary shops. Most were sold by the pound, such as aniseed for ten pence; labdanum, three shillings six pence; opium, twelve shillings; white wax, one shilling four pence; and Venice turpentine, six shillings. An ounce of oil of roses was a penny (about $1.66 in today's money), and rose water was sixteen pence for a pint. The most expensive, at two pounds ten shillings the ounce, was bezoar, an antidote to poison, reputed to be made of rare stones found in certain animals.

Metals and minerals were common ingredients in the prescriptions. Sixteenth-century wisdom claimed that gold had medicinal qualities, even the power of immortality. Mercury was already in use as an antidote to syphilis. Shavings of lead and tin were used, as were certain precious stones. Topaz and sapphires, for instance, are listed at twelve shillings per pound in *The Charitable Physitian*.

One writer claimed that quinces, like gold, had magical power. He urged pregnant women to eat quinces to have an intelligent child. (See the chapter "Care of Babies" for the recipe.) What was good for the head was apparently good for the body, because quinces were also recommended for several ailments in one prescription alone:

> Quinces are good for the stomach and to provoke urine, and are good against the dissentery and flux of the belly. Their decoction is singular

good to foment [apply a lotion to] the fundament [anus] or matrix [uterus] that cometh forth, and they are good against the inflammation of women's breasts [milk fever] and against vomitings.[5]

Today, because they are extremely high in pectin, they are considered an antidiarrhetic.

Snails were an ingredient in some home remedies. "Whole shell snails" or their oil were considered antidotes to snake bite in a 1577 remedy in *A Booke of Soveraigne Approved Medicines and Remedies*. Snails appear in a gout recipe mentioned below. Black snails formed the main ingredient in a medication to remove "corns on the feet or toes," and red snails were part of this remedy "For sore eyes":

Take red snails and seeth [boil] them in fair water, and then gather the oil that ariseth thereoff, and therewith anoint your eyes morning and evening.[6]

Snails were also supposed to be good "For a fellon [abscess]":

Take garden snails and beat them in a mortar, shells and bodies and all, till they be smooth and like an uniform unguent. Then apply this like a poultice, & when it beginneth to stink, (which it will do in few hours) change it. This will cure it in two or three days.[7]

Some of the homemade cures seem worse than the problems they treated. Many of them were also time-consuming to make. Take, for example, this recipe "For Pain in the Head" (and be glad you can take aspirin):

Take of the best salad oil you can get, & the flowers of wild primroses & put them into the oil, & then set it on the fire and let it boil half an hour very softly. Then put it in a glass & set it in the sun 3 weeks, and then rub your temples evening and morning.[8]

Here is "A Medicine for the Head Burning that Long Time Hath Been," but whether it was meant to cure a headache, a fever or both is hard to tell:

Take a quantity of the gall of a hare & as much of honey. Mingle it together a good while till it turn red, and with it anoint the forehead, and all the aching shall be taken away. This is a precious ointment.[9]

Many of the diseases that appear in sixteenth- and seventeenth-century literature are either unknown today or known by different names. They may also be variants of modern diseases. "Sweating sickness" or the "great English sweat," frequently fatal, was a mysterious flu-like disease that died out after the mid-sixteenth century; "lask" was the name for dysentery or diarrhea; the word leprosy was sometimes extended to other skin diseases; the "falling evil" was epilepsy; "quinsy" or "squinancy," a disease of the throat, may have been tonsillitis; "an ague" referred to a high, often cyclical fever (typhus or malaria), or the shivering or cold that frequently accompanied a severe fever; the "English itch" was usually scabies; the French pox meant syphilis; ringworm or a similar skin eruption was called a "tetter"; and dropsy was a condition marked by excessive thirst and liquid retention.

The old recipes tell a story of fearful diseases and ailments. Children and babies suffered from worms (see the chapter "Care of Babies" for two antidotes); injuries took their toll for lack of adequate sanitation and medicine; plague, smallpox, and other deadly diseases recurred with terrifying frequency; childbirth, with its hemorrhaging and infections, was a recurring risk; and lice, rats, and fleas (often carrying disease) were common if unwelcome visitors in almost any household. But the recipe books had remedies for these problems—and more.

Wounds and Accidents

The English Civil War in the 1640s resulted in countless wounded soldiers needing treatment, sometimes in country homes near battle-grounds. The hazards of strenuous everyday life brought more wounds and bleeding. Books of cures had many formulas for treating these problems. "To heal a wound within ten days as by proof hath been seen" is one:

Stamp camphor with barrow's [young castrated hog] grease, and put it into the wound, and it will heal it.[10]

Another, called "To Clean a Wound," said to "Take beer, wheat, stone flower and honey, boil it thick, apply it to."[11] "To Staunch Bleeding," at least from the nose, seemed to require a bit of magic:

> A very desperate and continual bleeding at the nose had often been staunched by making the party hold in their hand, or anywhere about their body, a little of the herb burfa pastoris. Wear it continually, and it will prevent bleeding. It will suffice, though one wear it but in their pocket or to their hatband.[12]

If clutching a remedy in the hand didn't stop the nosebleed, you could

> Burn an eggshell in the fire till it be as black as a coal. Then beat it to a fine powder, and let the party snuff it up into his nostrils.[13]

Two recipes used dung as a main ingredient to stop bleeding. "Lay hog's dung, hot from the hog, to the bleeding wound,"[14] said one. The second was the same except that it called for the addition of sugar to the dung.[15] Writers copied each other; a recipe in one book would be repeated without apology or acknowledgement in another. There was no stigma attached to plagiarism.

The dung of barnyard animals and birds (including doves, pigeons, horses, sheep, hogs, cows, and geese) appears often in recipes. Dung was sometimes referred to as a "filth" ingredient in remedies. Camel dung had been used in ancient times to make sal ammoniac (by distilling or burning it and using the soot). As late as the nineteenth century, American pioneers used buffalo dung in medications, claiming it had soothing qualities. Ammonia is used to this day for medicinal purposes—for example, as an antidote to bee stings. It may, then, have been the ammoniacal qualities of dung that proved useful in Early Modern England.

Dung was usually an ingredient in salves for the skin. It was also used for remedies taken internally, though usually only for extreme conditions. For example, with yellow jaundice,

> which is desperate and almost past cure, take sheep's dung new made and put it into a cup of beer or ale and close the cup fast and let it stand

so all night, and in the morning take a draught of the clearest of the drink, and give it unto the sick party.[16]

Or "To Prevent Marking in the Smallpox":

An infallible remedy for the same: In a wine glass full of sack [white wine or sherry] dissolve as much sheep's dung, newly taken out of the sheep's gut warm as will make it pretty thick, yet so that the patient may drink it.[17]

But topical use of dung was the norm. "An Oil to Help Hearing" consisted mainly of a gray eel with a white belly placed in a "deep hole in a horse dunghill," then covered with more dung, and left there two weeks before use.[18] Pigeon's dung (along with white wine vinegar, "the grease of a puppydog," parsley, and garden snails) was part of "Another Excellent Plaster for the Gout."[19] Goose dung was a main ingredient in a salve "For the canker in a woman's breast."[20] "For a Pain in the Back," fresh cow dung was recommended, fried in vinegar, and applied as a plaster to the back.[21] Dove's dung and red rose leaves, heated in a quilted bag, were recommended "To Help a Stitch in the Side or Elsewhere."[22]

Judging by the number of remedies for burns and scalds, cooking was a dangerous occupation. This recipe also uses dung:

Take goose dung and the middle bark of an elder tree. Fry them in May butter, strain them, and therewith anoint the burned or scalded place.[23]

Not all remedies for burns depended on dung, however:

Take of oil olive a pint, turpentine a pound, unwrought wax half a pound, resin a quarter of a pound, sheep's suet two pound. Then take of orpine, smallage, ragwort, plantain and sicklewort [plants], of each a good handful. Chop all the herbs very small and boil them in a pan altogether upon a soaking [slow] fire, and stir them exceeding much till they be well incorporate together. Then take it from the fire and strain all through a strong canvas cloth into clean pots or glasses, and use it as your occasion shall serve, either to anoint, taint or plaster.[24]

And "Lady Goring's Remedy for a Burn or Scald" instructed:

Take hog's fat or seam [hog's lard] made of it, melt it, but let it not boil. Put into it the white of a new laid egg or two well beaten, and stir it continually on embers till it be like an ointment. Keep it for your use, anointing the sore twice a day with it.[25]

This "Medicine for a Burn" is the simplest of all, as long as there is a nursing mother nearby: "Take oil of roses and woman's milk and put it into the open place, and it will heal it."[26]

Plagues and Scourges

When bubonic plague attacked Londoners, the royal court fled the city. Statutes were issued forbidding anyone from infected regions to enter Windsor Castle when the court took refuge there during severe plagues. For those left behind, several preventive measures could be taken. "A Medicine to be Used during all the Time of the Plague; Good against Infection" called again for a form of ammoniac.[27] But "Another Infallible Antidote" went it one further and called for urine:

Take a little, almost half a glassful of your own water (of the morning water), beat with two or three spoonfuls of it a little rue and a little ache (in French), aspium (in Latin) [wild celery or parsley] not half a handful of each. Squeeze out all their juice hard. Drink this wine and juice fasting. That morning you do so, you need not fear any infected house or persons.[28]

One book, *The Treatise of the Plague*, discussed all aspects of plague epidemics. Published in 1603, it speculated on the causes of the disease (long before the connection to rats and fleas was known) and suggested building separate hospitals for plague victims. It also recommended freshening sick rooms with sweet-smelling antidotes for infected air, as well as mild diets, preventive pills, protective measures for those who nursed victims, blood-letting, and certain household remedies—for example:

As soon therefore as anyone feeleth himself siezed, give him this potion. Take of the juice of marigolds, the quantity of two or three ounces, give it the patient to drink with a little white wine or sorrel water, and cover him well that he may sweat.[29]

"Sweetening"—or purifying—the air was considered important. This "Preventive Against the Plague" was one such air-freshener:

Divers good physicians' opinions are that to burn tar every morning in a chafing dish of coals is most excellent against the plague. Also put in a little wine vinegar to the tar. It is most excellent and approved.[30]

Markham offered his own preventives and cures for the plague. This antidote also describes plague symptoms and discomforts:

If you be infected with the plague and feel the assured signs thereof, as pain in the head, drought, burning, weakness of stomach and such like, then you shall take a dram of the best mithridate [universal antidote composed of many ingredients] and dissolve it in three or four spoonfuls of dragon water, and immediately drink it off, and then with hot cloths or bricks made extreme hot and laid to the soles of your feet, after you have been wrapped in woolen clothes, compel yourself to sweat, which if you do, keep yourself moderately therein till the sore begin to rise. Then to the same apply a live pigeon cut in two parts or else a plaster made of the yolk of an egg, honey, herb of grace [rue, an herb] chopped exceeding small, and wheat flower which in very short space will not only ripen but also break the same without any other incision. Then after it hath run a day or two you shall apply a plaster of melilot [a plant] unto it until it be whole.[31]

The Queens Closet Opened, first published a decade before the last plague epidemic and the great fire of London, continued in print many years after those catastrophes. It had nineteen long and detailed recipes for prevention or cure of the plague, though most are preventives. One claimed to be "The only receipt against the plague."[32] The bottom line, though, was to "Call upon God, desiring him to defend us."[33]

Although the plague was the worst scourge, there were lesser diseases for which equally questionnable cures were offered. For example, an "ague," a malaria-like fever recurring at regular intervals and accompanied by severe chills—along with its cousin, a "hot ague," which may have been typhus—while not as lethal as the plague, was yet common enough to warrant many prescriptions:

First take advice of your doctor; that will be, I know, to purge and let blood which indeed is a great preparation for obtaining of health in all diseases. . . . If your ague stick to you after you have been under your doctor's hands, take little pieces of alum, scrape and cut them to the fashion of pills, & let them that are very young, very old, or very weak take three of these alum pills in three spoonfuls of aniseed water. Let the stronger sort take five or six in the same manner. This is a remedy whereby I never failed to cure as many as ever I took in hand . . .[34]

Another remedy called for nutmeg, burnt alum, and white vinegar, mixed together and given "an hour before the fit."[35] As with many other illnesses, there was an antidote to be applied externally for those thought too weak or vulnerable for the stronger, internal medicine. "For the ague in children or women with child," the patient was to

Take Venice turpentine, spread it on the rough side of a piece of thin leather, two fingers breadth, and strow thereon the powder of frankincense finely beaten, and upon it some nutmeg grated. Bind this upon the wrists an hour before the fit comes, and renew it still till the fit be gone.[36]

One symptom of leprosy was a throat irritation; this was common to quinsy or squinancy as well and explains why there was a cure "For Leprosy and Squinancy":

Take a pint of the juice of houseleek and half a pint of verjuice. With these and a pint and a half of milk make posset drink of which give half a pint in the morning and as much at night. But to do better, be drinking of it all day long, so that you drink up this proportion in twenty-four hours. It cureth the leprosy, the squinancy, the painful white swellings in the knees and any aches.[37]

Heart attacks, common in the Western world today, were less common three and four hundred years ago. Few household remedies related specifically to the heart. This one, "Against the trembling of the heart," did:

Take 3 or 4 spoonfuls of claret wine and half as much damask rosewater, an ounce of white sugar-candy dissolved, and give it the sick to drink warm.[38]

Smallpox was confused with measles at times, often at its onset; some cures for the one were considered cures for the other. Chicken pox, or "varicella," does not enter the literature until the eighteenth century, at least by that name. Here is a dual antidote "For the smallpox or measles":

> Take an ounce of treacle, half an ounce of set wall [possibly wallflower], cut small, a penniworth of saffron ground small. Mix them and take thereof in a morning upon a knive's point as much as you can take up at twice or thrice, three mornings together.[39]

As for measles and smallpox in children, one midwifery book made this strange analysis of the diseases:

> The cause of both of them are the relics of the impurer part of the blood wherewith the child was nourished in his mother's womb which now is separated and thrust to the skin through the help and strength of nature . . . though the child be nourished with the best part of the menstrual blood, yet there remains some little portion behind which is of an ill quality, and after the child is born and is grown strong, he, gathering together his forces and natural heat, thrusts it forth by the pores of the skin.[40]

Smallpox was not just a childhood disease, as many adults learned to their horror. There were some attempts at cures for this killer, including a "Medicine to drive out the smallpox":

> Take of distilled tarragon water eight spoonfuls, and put thereto six grains of bezoar [poison antidote] or unicorns' horns, or for want of those two, put so much saffron, but the other is better. Let it be warm, double the portion as you see cause, taking nothing an hour before, nor an hour after.[41]

When the pocks turned out to be measles, there was this remedy:

> Take julep of violets two ounces, rose water four ounces, oil of vitriol four grains. Mix them and let it be drunk cold. This is a most rare medicine.[42]

Should these measures fail, the patient could try a number of suggestions to prevent scarring—including the one using sheep's dung mentioned in the chapter "Face and Fashion," and this one (if you owned a red cow), "To take away the pock-holes or any spot in the face":

> Take white rose water and wet a fine cloth therein, and set it all night to freeze, and then lay it upon your face till it be dry. Also take three poppies, the reddest you can get, and quarter them, taking out the garbage, then still them in a quart of new milk of a red cow, and with the water thereof wash your face.[43]

For epilepsy, or "the falling evil," there was this curious remedy:

> For the falling evil take, if it be a man, a female mole; if a woman, a male mole, and take them in March or else April when they go to the buck [copulate]. Then dry it in an oven and make powder of it whole as you take it out of the earth. Then give the sick person of the powder to drink evening and morning for nine or ten days together.[44]

Dropsy, the "bloating sickness," had various cures. This one, "An Approved Medicine for the Dropsy," was sandwiched between food and drink recipes in *The Ladies Cabinet Opened* in 1639:

> Take the herb called bittersweet (it groweth in waters and bears a purple flower), slice the stalks and boil a pretty deal of them in white wine, and drink thereof, first and last, morning and evening, and it will cure the dropsy.[45]

Another cure for dropsy called for red mint, "blind nettles" (nettles without the stinging quality of the common weed), and red sage stamped together in ale instead of white wine. It concluded, "and (God willing) it will do away your disease."[46] Again the fallback position: it's in God's hands.

Stones (usually kidney or bladder) were common, given that there were at least a dozen cures for them in one tome, *A Booke of Soveraigne Approved Medicines and Remedies*. One was listed as "A medicine against the stone in the back or bladder, or for the weakness of the back, which is called the running of the reins." Another book made two suggestions in the same paragraph "for the violent pain of the stone":

> Make a posset of milk and sack, then take off the curd, and put a handful of camomile flowers into the drink, then put it into a pewter pot and

let it stand upon hot embers so that it may dissolve, and then drink it as occasion shall serve. Other for this grief, take the stone of an oxgall [ox gallstone] and dry it in an oven, then beat it to powder, and take of it the quantity of a hazlenut with a draught of good old ale or white wine.[47]

Gout, too, was common, if the number of printed remedies are a guide. *The Booke of Soveraigne Approved Medicines and Remedies* alone offered half a dozen lengthy recipes, and there were two in *The Ladies Cabinet Opened*. One of them, "An Approved Medicine for the Gout in the Feet," suggested:

Take an ox's paunch, new killed and warm out of the belly, about the latter end of May or beginning of June. Make two holes therein, and put in your feet, and lay store of warm clothes about it, to keep it warm so long as can be. Use this three or four days together for three weeks or a month, whether you have the fit or pain of the gout at that time or no, so you have had it at any time before. This hath cured diverse persons that they have never been troubled with it again.[48]

The other was called "A Poltice for the Gout":

Take new milk, white bread grated and an handful of red rose leaves. Boil them together to the thickness of a poltice, then spread them on a linen cloth, and apply them to the place grieved.[49]

Remedies for the same problem were often very different, not just slight variations on a similar cure, as can be seen from these few samples. Despite the variety, there were in fact few effective cures to be had.

Poisons and Poisonous Bites

England was host to the poisonous adder snake and numerous wild animals whose bites could be dangerous. Antidotes were available, but hardly infallible. Sometimes the same cure was recommended for both poisons and bites, as in "A present certain cure of any poison inward or outward, or for the stinging of venomous beasts in men or beasts":

Take the leaves of black currants in powder one dram. Give it in wine or anything. It is a present remedy. You may gather the leaves in summer and keep them dry all the year.[50]

The Ladies Cabinet Enlarged and Opened recommended an external remedy "to cure the biting of all venomous beasts" that used, instead of black currant leaves, mustard mixed with vinegar or the milk of green fig leaves.[51] And there was "an approved remedy for biting of a mad dog" that used tin shavings:

Take a quart of ale and a dram of treacle, a handful of rue, a spoonful of shavings or filings of tin. Boil these all together till half be consumed. Take of this two spoonfuls in the morning and at night cold. It is excellent for man or beast.[52]

Lesser Ailments

Day-to-day irritants also confronted housewives, such as toothaches, coughs, bad breath, bed-wetting, constipation, insomnia, hemorrhoids, "tetters" (skin disorders), and indigestion—minor health problems much like those we suffer today, for which the services of a doctor were, then and now, often unnecessary. The old remedies, though, were quite different.

Dentistry was unknown, and the best solution for an aching tooth was to yank it out. But several seventeenth-century books did offer preventive measures, as well as recipes for cleaning the teeth and mouth. This one, "To make teeth white," is in a 1649 book by the man who coauthored the book with the frontispiece used in this chapter. He may have been a quack, but the recipe is not as bad as some:

Take vinegar of squills [a bulbous herb] and dip a little piece of a linen rag in it and rub the teeth and gums therewith. This also fasteneth the gums, comforteth the roots of the teeth and maketh a sweet breath.[53]

Another suggestion, this one from *The Queens Closet Opened,* might have merit today:

If you will keep your teeth from rotting or aching, wash the mouth continually every morning with juice of lemons, and afterward rub your teeth with a sage leaf, and wash your teeth after meat with fair water.[54]

But this recipe, "To take away the cause of the pain in the teeth," from *The Ladies Cabinet Opened,* seems optimistic (though the wine might help):

Wash the mouth two or three times together in a morning every month with white wine wherein the root of spurge [an euphorbium] hath been sodden [boiled], and you shall never have pain in your teeth.[55]

Still another way "To cure the tooth-ache," again from *The Queen's Closet Opened*, required a strong belief in magic. The writer claimed, "The tooth of a dead man carried about a man presently suppresses the pains of the teeth."[56] If the problem persisted and the tooth had to come out, there was a remedy (again using spurge) "to make a tooth fall out of itself":

Take wheat flour and mix it with the milk of an herb called spurge. Make thereof a paste and fill the hole of the tooth therewith and leave it there, changing it every two hours, and the tooth will fall out.[57]

If bad breath was a problem, *The Closet for Ladies and Gentlewomen* offered a fragrant remedy called "Against a stinking breath":

Take rosemary leaves with the blossoms, if you can get them, and seeth them in white wine with a little myrrhe and cinnamon, and you shall find a marvelous effect, if you use it often in your mouth.[58]

"A medicine for a cough" in the same book said to "take mustard seeds & put it into figs & seeth it in ale & drink it."[59] It also had a solution "For one that speaketh in his sleep":

Take southernwood [aromatic plant with a sour taste] & temper it with wine and let the diseased drink thereof in the morning and when he goeth to bed.[60]

If the problem was insomnia, *A Booke of Soveraigne Approved Medicines and Remedies* counseled:

Take a spoonful of oil of roses, a spoonful of rose water and half a spoonful of red vinegar, and temper them all together. Then with a fine linen cloth anoint the patient's head.[61]

The Queens Closet Opened had two ways "to procure sleep":

Bruise a handful of aniseeds and steep them in red rose water, and make it up in little bags, and bind one of them to each nostril, and it will cause sleep.[62]

(Or asphyxiation.) And:

Chop camomile and crumbs of brown bread small, and boil them with white wine vinegar. Stir it well and spread it on a cloth and bind it to the soles of the feet as hot as you can suffer it. You may add to it dried red rose leaves or red rose cakes with some red rose water, and let it heat till it be thick, and bind some of it to the temples, and some to the soles of the feet.[63]

The same book had "A Receipt to Help Digestion":

Take two quarts of small ale. Put to it red mints one handful, as much of red sage, a little cinnamon. Let it boil softly till half be wasted, sweeten it with sugar to your taste, and drink thereof a draught morning and evening.[64]

There was "A medicine for the itch":

Take sweet butter and unwrought wax and brimstone and a little rose water, red clove water. Boil them together till they be like a salve. Then anoint your body and arms and legs all over, three times by the fire therewith and no more.[65]

"An excellent good medicine or salve for any ache coming of cold, easy to be made by any country goodhousewife" appeared in the 1639 *Ladies Cabinet Opened* (next to a recipe for preserving barberries) and was repeated in the 1654 *Ladies Cabinet Enlarged and Opened*:

Take of good neatsfoot oil, honey and new wax a like quantity. Boil them well together. Then put to them a quarter so much of aqua vitae as was of each of the other, and then, setting it on the fire, boil it till they be well incorporated together. Then spread it upon a piece of thin leather or thick linen cloth, and so apply it to the place pained.[66]

These books also had a remedy "For the scall or scabbiness of the head":

Take of red sage, woodbine leaves and ground ivy a like quantity, in all so much as a good handful. Boil them in a pint of hog's grease, a quarter of an hour. Then strain the medicine from the herbs into a gallipot, and therewith anoint the head.[67]

And they offered "a medicine that hath healed old sores upon the legs that have run so long that the bones have been seen":

Take a quantity of good sweet cream and as much brimstone [sulphur], beaten in fine powder as will make it thick like paste. "Then take so much sweet butter as will work it into the form of an ointment, and herewith anoint the place grieved twice a day.[68]

If hemorrhoids or piles developed, *The English House-wife* offered several solutions, including:

Take half a pint of ale and a good quantity of pepper and as much alum as a walnut. Boil all this together till it be as thick as birdlime or thicker. This done, take the juice of white violets and the juice of houseleek, and when it is almost cold, put in the juice and strain them all together, and with this ointment anoint the sore place twice a day. Otherwise for this grief take lead and grate it small, and lay it upon the sores, or else take mussels, dried and beat to powder, and lay it on the sores.[69]

According to *The Ladies Cabinet Opened*, one way to solve constipation was to use "A clyster [enema] to open and loosen the body being bound, which may safely be ministered to any man or woman":

Take mallows and mercury, unwashed, of each two handfuls, half a handful of barley, clean rubbed and washed. Boil them in a pottle [half-gallon measure] of running water to a quart. Then strain out the water and put it in a skillet, and put to it three spoonfuls of salad oil, two spoonfuls of honey and a little salt. Then make it lukewarm, and so minister it.[70]

A Closet for Ladies and Gentlewomen had a different idea on how "to keep one laxative":

> Take a new laid egg, put out the white, then put in new butter, unsalted, heat it. Then eat it, use it often.[71]

To give a clyster, or enema, required an enema bag or, as it was called then, a "syringe" or "bladder." *The Charitable Physitian* listed "those instruments which the rich ought to have in their houses." High on the list were:

> Two syringes or bladders fitted with pipes to give clysters, the one for great folks, and the other for children. A little brass pot to keep a clyster in, and to warm it in. Another bladder and box pipe to lend charitably to the poor.[72]

The book warned that if the clyster equipment was loaned to anyone with the plague or other deadly disease, it should be well washed before the next use. This was hardly adequate sanitation, but it was a step toward recognizing the infectious nature of some illnesses. *The Charitable Physitian* had eighteen recipes for enemas in a chapter on "The manner to make clysters," including one "against the beginning of the dysentery." The book also had a price list for simples and home medical equipment. And there were over two pages of "medicaments which the rich ought to have in their homes." Almost nothing on the list would be found in a twentieth-century medicine cabinet except the "quantity of pills." It included:

> 4 ounces of good Agaricke
> 4 ounces of diaphanicum
> A quantity of pills of three or four sorts
> Four pound of good common honey
> Half a pound of syrup of poppies
> An ounce of pellitory
> Four ounces of Azarum root
> Half a pound of red rose leaves and as many violets
> A dram of good bezoar
> Four ounces of white wax
> A pound of oil of quinces[73]

The English Unparalell'd Physitian and Chyrurgian, though not addressed specifically to women, was dedicated to the rich, the "middle sort," the poor, and "physitians and chyrurgians," and probably found its way into the hands of many housewives. Among its remedies were two for tetters. One, "For a tetter or ringworm," involved anointing the diseased skin with "syrup of sugar" to bring the worms to the surface. The other, "A man cured that was full of tetters," said:

This was the manner of his cure. He took the rennet [stomach membrane] of a calf and drank it in milk three or four times, and sweat thereupon. Then he anointed the parts affected with saccharum saturni [lead acetate] mixed with oil of roses warm.[74]

The same book had a "cure of the gonorrhea or running of the reins, the forerunner of the foul disease":

First you shall give them aromatico once in white wine. Then morning and evening for seven or eight days, use this potion following, anointing also the reins and those parts with *aquae faetida*,[75] being cold, and in short time they shall be healed. Take the whites of four or five new laid eggs, two ounces of fine sugar, three ounces of rose water. Mix them well, and drink it morning and evening. This is a rare secret and often proved. The drink must be drunk cold.[76]

The prostate could trouble a man then as now, though fewer men survived to an age when it could cause major problems. Some remedies made their way into books, such as one "To Loose and Purge the Urine Stopped in a Man" in *A Booke of Sovereigne Approved Medicines*:

Take of English saffron beaten to fine powder, and of pure black soap equal portions, and being well mingled together, spread it upon a plaster of leather . . . then lay it upon the navel of the sick, and it shall help the avoidance of the urine within an hour.[77]

To strengthen a "weak or diseased" back, the *Ladies Cabinet* books suggested:

Take the pith of an ox's back, wash it in wine or ale, and beating it very small, strain it through a coarse cloth, and make a caudle of it with muscadine or strong ale. Boil therein a few dates, sliced and the stones taken out, and drink it first and last as warm as you can, walking well but temperately after it. Toasted dates often eaten are very good for the same.[78]

The cures for these lesser ailments followed the general formula of superstition mixed with magic and rather arbitrary ingredients. Meanwhile, physicians favored blood-letting, which, unfortunately, caused weakening and infection in many of their patients. It was not, however, a measure often used by female healers. But the human body can overcome many errors—especially if the mind believes in the remedy or the practitioner.

Snake Oil

The term "snake oil" conjures up pictures of unsavory salesmen pushing bottles of cure-alls on gullible pioneers in nineteenth-century America. But snake oil has been around for centuries. And much of it actually contained oil from snakes.

That versatile little book *The Ladies Cabinet Enlarged and Opened* had two recipes. In the first, "How to make oil of snakes and adders," the book merely claims, "This oil doth wonderful cures in recovering hearing in those that be deaf;" and if a few drops are put in a defective ear, "It's reported that some have been cured that were born deaf by using this oil." To make it,

> Take snakes or adders [the one poisonous snake of the British Isles] when they are fat, which will be in June or July, cut off their heads and take off their skins, and unbowel them, and put them into a glass gourd, and pour out so much of the pure spirit of wine well rectified, that it may cover them four or five fingers breadth, stop the glass well, and set it in balneo [vessel of hot water] till all their substance be turned into an oil, which keep well stopped for your use.[79]

The other recipe, "Quintessence of snakes, adders, or vipers," was much the same, except that it called for more wine to be added to the oil. But it promised much grander cures, concluding:

> This quintessence is of extraordinary virtue to purify the blood, flesh and skin, and consequently all diseases therein. It cures the falling

sickness, strengthens the brain, sight and hearing, and preserveth from gray hairs, reneweth youth, preserveth women from abortion, cureth the gout, consumption, causeth sweat, is very good in and against pestilential infections.[80]

The wine, at least, could numb the pain. Two authors actually poked fun at themselves in a cartoon frontispiece (reproduced at the beginning of this chapter) showing two men trying to hoodwink an audience into buying their cure-all. The writers, Salvator Winter and Francisco (or Francis) Dickinson, claimed to be "expert operators" of Italian background. Together in 1649 they authored *A Pretious Treasury or a New Dispensatory.* (This is the book with the cartoon.) In the same year Dickinson wrote separately *A Pretious Treasury of Twenty Rare Secrets*, and Winter offered *A New Dispensatory of Fourty Physicall Receipts*, a short nine pages of remedies that concluded with extravagant claims for his prowess in dental work:

> Furthermore I pull out all manner of hollow teeth, stumps or roots, with great dexterity and ease without almost any pain. I make teeth smooth and white, set in artificial ones that they shall not be discerned from the natural ones . . . and I know none shall go beyond me in that art.[81]

The books were not identical, but some remedies were repeated; all required extraordinary faith in the authors. Almost one hundred years earlier, Queen Mary had empowered the president of the Royal College of Physicians to imprison charlatans who sold "evil and faulty stuff."[82] Regardless, quacks continued to thrive. Dickinson disappears after 1649, but Winter resurfaced fifteen years later as the author of *Directions for the Use of My Elixir, My Philosophicall Petza or Plaister, My Balsom and also My Purging Drink.* Far from punished, Winter claimed in the fourth edition of his elixir book that he was publishing it "by his Majesty's Authority," and it was

> of such admirable virtue that it alone is sufficient not only to cure any disease incident unto man and to prolong even old age itself, but to prevent any disease from fixing upon you.[83]

Many readers must have suspected that the remedies were not as reliable as the salesmen might claim. Regardless, naivete persisted, and "doctors" continued to advertise themselves and their pills in short, printed leaflets, each declaring his superiority. One example is "Jones of Hatton Garden," who made extravagant claims for his doctoring ability and printed a long list of the names and addresses of people he cured, then announced he was available from nine to five for consultations.[84] These men were undoubtedly quacks, encroaching not only on members of the College of Physicians but also on female healers, at least in the city of London.

Waters

The distilling of various waters was a standard activity in any well-run household. Distilling assured the product's purity. It involved (besides a great deal of patience) a specially chambered pot, called an "alembic" or "limbeck," in which water was boiled and the steam condensed and drawn off into a side vessel. (See frontispiece to "Preparing Food.")

There are many references to stillrooms and alembics, but little was written on just how the procedure worked. Perhaps this paragraph, "Of the distillation of waters" from *The Charitable Physitian*, explains:

> For the distilling of simple waters, everyone hath knowledge as to put the herbs being bruised or picked into a still and covering of it, keeping a moderate fire. Also for the stilling of flowers or herbs in a limbeck putt[ing] water unto them and putting cold water in the top, and drawing away the first water which is the strength, and throwing away the rest. Therefore we shall not need to write any more of this.[85]

Distilling was time-consuming for the housewife. The opening directions in the following recipe, "To make sweet water," were demanding enough (collecting "a thousand damask roses" was no mean feat in itself). Then the direction "distill it" required more time and skill, but—in common with most such recipes—the process was not described:

> To make sweet water of the best kind, take a thousand damask roses, two good handfuls of lavendar tops, a three penny weight of mace, two

ounces of cloves bruised, a quart of running water. Put a little water into the bottom of an earthen pot, and then put in your roses and lavendar with the spices by little and little [little by little], and in the putting in always knead them down with your fist, and so continue it until you have wrought up all your roses and lavendar, and in the working between put in always a little of your water. Then stop your pot close and let it stand four days, in which time every morning and evening put in your hand and pull from the bottom of your pot the said roses, working it for a time, and then distill it, and hand in the glass of water a grain or two of musk wrapped in a piece of sarcenet or fine cloth.[86]

Cleaners, Dyers, and Insecticides

Along with waters, salves, medicines, and other remedies, a house-wife was expected to keep on hand such household essentials as soaps, spot removers, dyes, and insecticides. Recipes for all of them were available in the books men produced.

The Treasury of Hidden Secrets had what seems even today a sensible recipe that "Taketh off all staining, dying and spots from the hands of artificers that get them by working and maketh them white and fair":

Take the juice of a lemon with a little bay-salt and wash your hands with it, and let them dry of themselves. Wash them again, and you shall find all the spots and staining gone. It is also very good against the scurffe [scurvy] or scabs.[87]

An antidote to oil and grease spots used ashes:

Take the bones of sheep's feet, burn them almost to ashes, then bruise them to powder, and put of it upon your spots, and lay all before the sun when it shines hottest. When the powder becomes black, lay on fresh in the place till it suck out the spots, which is done in very short time.[88]

Basic soap recipes called for animal lard and ashes. Fancy, aromatic soap could be made by taking plain, finished soap and adding these ingredients:

Take storax [resin] of both kinds, Benjamin, Calamus, Aromaticus, Labdanum of each a like, and bray them [pound with a pestle] to powder with cloves and arras. Then beat them all with a sufficient quantity of soap till it be stiff. Then with your hand you shall work it like paste and make round balls thereof.[89]

Cloth was sometimes dyed at home, using various natural coloring agents, though professional dyers had a greater variety of dyes and the mordants to set them. This recipe is "to die wool blue":

Take good store of old chamber lye [urine, a common ingredient in dyes] and set it on the fire. Then take half a pound of blue neale [deep-blue dye] and beat it small in a mortar, and then put it into the lye, and when it seeths [boils] put in your wool.[90]

Lice were a menace, judging by the number of recipes for eliminating the pesky creatures. Here is one of several from the 1544 *Booke of Children*: "Take mustard and dissolve it in vinegar with a little salt peter, and anoint the places where as the lice are wont to breed."[91] And another, from the 1628 *Booke of Pretty Conceits*:

Make a good fire and put quicksilver [mercury] therein, and hang the clothes that are troubled with lice over the fire in the smoke, and then assure yourself no vermin will breed or come in them.[92]

The same book had "An easy way to kill fleas":

Take the herb coriander and seethe it well in water, and then sprinkle the same water in your chambers and rooms, and it will destroy all the fleas.[93]

In 1649 the lice were still around, and one suggestion was made "How any that in necessity are troubled with lice or any other vermin may destroy them suddenly":

Take laurel oil half an ounce, three penny worth of quick silver. Mingle them well and anoint therewith the places where you have most vermin, and you shall be suddenly clear from all such things.[94]

Rats and fleas were a plague in any household long before scientists discovered their fatal connection. There were recipes for getting rid of them, but fewer than for lice. This one, from the 1628 *Booke of Pretty Conceits*, has shades of the Pied Piper about it:

> Take a quick rat, and put her in a pot, and make fire about it and under it. And when she feeleth the heat she will cry, and the rats that hear her will come to help her, and then they [you] may take them. And in like manner you may do with moles.[95]

The old cures quoted here may seem odd, even horrifying to modern minds. To this day, however, home remedies—somewhat improved—still make up a popular subset of medical treatment in the United States. It is tempting to laugh at our ancestors' so-called cures and declare modern medicine vastly superior. Yet there are today many problems—from deadly diseases like cancer and AIDS to the common cold and acne—that defy our best minds. When public trust in the medical profession falters and the cost of health care soars, people still turn to their own devices. In the late twentieth century a flowering of health-food stores, books, and newsletters, as well as personal health columns in newspapers and magazines, attract the health-conscious consumer. All kinds of odd—and often suspect—advice is offered, much as in the sixteenth and seventeenth centuries. Of course, some of these homemade remedies happen to work—just as some were helpful in earlier times.

Folk medicine is still alive and well. Some columnists encourage readers to submit their favorite remedies. A 1987 article in the *New York Times* discussed canker sores and the mystery of why they come and go. One reader replied that almonds were causing her canker sores; another advised eating "six or eight almonds and within hours, or maybe minutes, the soreness will be gone." Tetracycline, vitamin C, wet tea bags, yogurt, buttermilk, hydrogen peroxide, baking soda, aloe-vera juice, milk of magnesia, and powdered alum have all been suggested by readers, among them doctors and lay "healers." The tannin in tea bags is the main ingredient in an over-the-counter medicine for canker sores. But this paragraph from the *Times* article might have been written about a centuries-old, quack remedy:

In other cases, the cure sounded worse than the disease. This proposal came from a Chicago reader: "Take 100 milligrams of nicotinic acid at the outset, and place a piece of lemon on the sore." Anyone who has had a canker sore knows that lemon is a sure route to searing pain.[96]

What did seventeenth-century home remedy books suggest for cankers? Here is one answer from *The Ladies Cabinet Englarged and Opened*—no better or worse than some of the twentieth-century ideas:

For the Canker in the Mouth: Take the juice of plantain [an herb, not the banana], vinegar and rosewater, of each a like quantity, mingle them together, and wash the mouth often with them.[97]

An article in the *Los Angeles Times* in 1988 discussed the flu going around that winter and the cures different people used. One person suggested:

I make up a batch of my mother's favorite hot toddy recipe—a large shot of Scotch with sugar and some tea. It may not cure me, but I don't feel the pain.

Another reader, quoted in the same article, nursed her flu with her grandmother's brew of boiled grapefruit juice and rind. Asked if there was some magical ingredient, she answered,

My fantasy is that it's quinine in the grapefruit rind, but a doctor might refute that. All I know is that it makes me feel better. And at night I put Scotch in the brew, and it really makes a difference.[98]

Sixteenth- and seventeenth-century housewives didn't put Scotch in their brews, but they were generous with wine, ale, and distilled herbal waters (which may have had a high alcoholic content).

The home-cure trend lately has found its way onto the Information Superhighway, not always a bastion of scientific rectitude. Certain Internet health-care discussion groups have attracted controversy because group members swap odd or untested cures for HIV, cancer, and other ailments. "Anybody with an opinion can post anything in a Usenet newsgroup, whether they know what they're talking about or not," declares Patrick Crispen, author of "Roadmap," an Internet training course.[99]

❦

Huge strides have been made in the twentieth century in eliminating diseases—controlling many with antibiotics, vaccines, and improved sanitation—and in perfecting surgical procedures. Yet new ailments arise. They and older, stubborn ones are still treated with kitchen remedies. And one has the nagging thought that chemicals used in prescriptions today may, in future centuries, be thought to be quite as bizarre as the metals, minerals, and excreta added to sixteenth- and seventeenth-century medications.

Women, according to men physicians in the sixteenth and seventeenth centuries, were to leave doctoring alone. But there were plenty of laymen and translators who produced medical guidebooks for the women's use. By the end of the century, middle-class women began to publish their own work—midwives, like Jane Sharp, and writers of practical guides, like Hannah Wolley. Despite male criticism, women healers continued to care for the day-to-day physical problems of families and rural communities. They tried to meet the need by writing down and passing on "old wives' tales" and cures that had circulated for centuries. A few of these handwritten recipes, remedies, and records found their way into early printed material published by men for women's use. While an aura of ancient superstition and magic attached to some remedies, people still relied on them. Today one might conclude such trust was misplaced. But how much worse were those remedies than the classical theories and blood-letting of the professional physicians? Sadly, neither the doctors nor the guidebook writers could offer much real help in time of illness and accident. As so many of the recipes said, a remedy would work, "God willing."

Some men were spreading dour threats about the inadequacies of female doctoring; others were cashing in by publishing remedy books for a female audience. Many of the surviving household remedy books are well worn with leaves frayed and candle burns scarring the pages. These books reveal that the treatment of medical problems was still part of ordinary domestic life—and thus part of the woman's role.

By organizing and mystifying their profession, the physicians succeeded—by the end of the seventeenth century—in elevating the public's regard for their abilities. But they did not succeed in taking over all medical practice. In 1680 one physician, known by his initials, T. K., finally broke ranks and signed his name to a medical book, *The Kitchen-Physician: Or a Guide for Good-Housewives in Maintaining Their Families in Health*, in which he explained:

> My design is (though bred up a physician) to leave this [book] as a legacy to my country . . . purely to make them their own physicians in cases not [too serious]
> . . . . I would not have the reader think that I have the least ill opinion of the elaborate inventions and ingenious experiments of the learned . . . , but I am not of opinion that their assistance is necessary in common and ordinary distempers which many times the diligent nurse or housewife by her plain and common experience and herbs and plants, cures when they by their sublime and too high strained applications, leave the patient in a desperate condition.[100]

This doctor, at least, was willing to share the healing profession with housewives who, regardless of outcries from most of the male profession, continued to serve as hands-on healers and midwives. ❦

Notes

1. Sir Arthur Salisbury MacNalty, *The Renaissance and its Influence on English Medicine, Surgery and Public Health* (1946), 21.
2. Juan Luis Vives, *The Instruction of a Christen Woman* (1529?), 108.
3. Philibert Guibert, *The Charitable Physitian with the Charitable Apothecary* (1639), A3.
4. Ibid., A3ᵛ.
5. Ibid., 159.
6. Gervase Markham, *The English House-wife* (1631), 20. This book appeared first in 1615 as *The English Huswife* in Markham's *Country Contentments*.
7. Sir Kenelm Digby, *Choice and Experimented Receipts in Physick and Chirurgery* (1668), 109–10.
8. *A Closet for Ladies and Gentlewomen* (1611), 98.
9. Ibid, 119.
10. *A Booke of Sovereigne Approved Medicines . . .* (1577), C1.
11. *Closet . . .* , 143.
12. Digby, 48.
13. *The Ladies Cabinet Opened* (1639), 12; M. B. *The Ladies Cabinet Enlarged and Opened* (1654), 88.
14. Samuel Strangehopes, *A Book of Knowledge* (1675), 78.
15. *Closet . . .* , 78.
16. Markham, 26.
17. Digby, 57.
18. Markham, 14.
19. Digby, 102.
20. *Ladies Cabinet . . .* , 14.
21. Strangehopes, 79.
22. Markham, 25.
23. W. M., *The Queens Closet Opened* (1661), 104.
24. Markham, 47.
25. W. M., 162.
26. *Closet . . .* , 180.
27. Ibid., 123.
28. Digby, 81.
29. Thomas Lodge, *A Treatise of the Plague* (1603), G4ᵛ.
30. W. M., 40.

31. Markham, 10.
32. W. M., 107.
33. Lodge, G4^v.
34. Francis Dickinson, *A Pretious Treasury of Twenty Rare Secrets* (1649), A3^v.
35. Salvator Winter, *A New Dispensatory of Fourty Physical Receipts* (1649), 11.
36. *Ladies Cabinet . . .* , 11.
37. Digby, 88.
38. John Murrell, *A Delightful Daily Exercise for Ladies and Gentlewomen* (1621), F7^v.
39. W. M., 29.
40. James Guillemeau, *Child-birth or, the Happy Deliverie of Women* (1612), 99.
41. W. M., 140.
42. M. B., 116.
43. *Closet . . .* , 130.
44. Markham, 14.
45. *Ladies Cabinet . . .* , 42.
46. M. B., 100.
47. Markham, 35.
48. *Ladies Cabinet . . .* , 34.
49. Ibid.
50. Digby, 50.
51. M. B., 108.
52. Digby, 114.
53. Winter, 8.
54. W. M., 191.
55. *Ladies Cabinet . . .* , 14.
56. W. M., 192.
57. *Ladies Cabinet . . .* , 14; M. B., 141. Many of the recipes in these two books are identical, but on different pages.
58. *Closet . . .* , 152.
59. Ibid., 178.
60. Ibid., 190.
61. *Booke of Soveraigne . . .* , C6^v.
62. W. M., 60.
63. Ibid., 101.
64. Ibid., 6.
65. Strangehopes, 78.

66. *Ladies Cabinet . . .* , 11; M. B., 83.

67. Ibid., 28, 129.

68. Ibid., 17; 133.

69. Markham, 38.

70. *Ladies Cabinet . . .* , 16.

71. *Closet . . .* , 144.

72. Guibert, 41.

73. Ibid., 41–44.

74. Daniel Border,*The English Unparalell'd Physitian and Chyrurgian* (1651), 14.

75. Aquae faetida, according to George Hocking's *Dictionary of Terms in Pharmacognosy* (Springfield, Ill.: Charles Thomas, 1955), is a distillation in alcohol of several herbs and roots including asafetida, a smelly gum from any of several roots with anti-spasmodic qualities. After removing the roots, patients would drink a quart of the "medication." If that didn't work, they could drink more. After a while they would certainly "feel no pain."

76. Border, 69.

77. *Booke of Soveraigne . . .* , CIII.

78. *Ladies Cabinet . . .* , 11; M. B., 85.

79. M. B., 76.

80. Ibid., 61–62.

81. Winter, 15.

82. W. S. C. Copeman, *Doctors and Disease in Tudor Times* (London: Dawson's of Pall Mall, 1960), 26.

83. Winter, *Directions for the Use of My Elixir* (1664), A.

84. Jones of Hatton Garden, *His Book of Cures* (1673), 1.

85. Guibert, 136.

86. Markham, 118.

87. *The Treasury of Hidden Secrets, Commonly Called, the Good-Huswives Closet* (1659), G.

88. Dickinson, A3[v].

89. Markham, *The English Huswife* in *Country Contentments* (1615), 80.

90. Ibid., 85.

91. Thomas Phaer, *The Boke of Chyldren* (1544), 64[v], printed with Jehan Goeurot, tr. Thomas Phaer, *The Regiment of Lyfe* (1544).

92. *The Booke of Pretty Conceits* (1628), B3.

93. Ibid., B3[v].

94. Dickinson, A3.

95. *Booke of Pretty Conceits*, B2[v].

96. Jane E. Brody, "Home Remedies for Sores" in *The New York Times*, Sept. 9, 1987.

97. M. B., 91.

98. Nikki Finke, "Flu Sissies and Stoics: How We Suffer" in *Los Angeles Times*, Feb. 10, 1988, Part V.

99. Patrick Crispen, Roadmap (Univ. of Alabama: listserv@uaivm.ua.edu, 1995), Map 8: Usenet.

100. T. K., *The Kitchen Physician: Or, a Guide for Good Housewives in Maintaining Their Families in Health* (1680), A2^v.

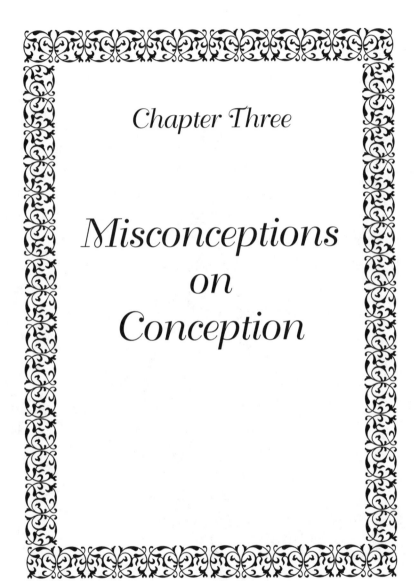

Chapter Three

Misconceptions
on
Conception

Misconceptions on Conception

"Where do babies come from?" Everyone wants to know at some time. Few questions are more fundamental. Yet for almost all of Western history the answers have been wrong.

Granted, the so-called civilized world has no problem with the fact that babies result from sexual intercourse, but what really goes on internally to create a new life has eluded humankind until modern times and is still a subject of study and discovery. The answers scholars and physicians came up with in the past not only were substantially wrong, they also created other wrongs that militated against females. These misconceptions on human conception contributed to the idea that women were not the equals of men. Religious and civil law, reflecting sexual bias about reproductive functions, reinforced the power of males and the subjugation of females.

Part of the blame lies with Aristotle. The ancient Greek thinker, widely regarded as one of the great sages of the Western world, erred on the sex question. Unfortunately, his theory of human reproduction, wrong as it was, stuck for almost 2,000 years.

Aristotle believed in a hierarchy that placed men above women. His theory of reproduction followed that theme. Aristotle taught that only the male produced the vital seed for new life. By his account, the woman's role was a passive one. She received the seed and "baked" it in her "oven,"

Opposite page:
CHILDBIRTH WITH ASTROLOGERS IN ATTENDANCE, from *De Conceptu et Generatione Hominis*, by Jakob Rüff (London, 1580). By permission of the Folger Shakespeare Library.

adding less important ingredients to the form and soul that the man had created. Aristotle's analysis is, of course, much more involved and complicated than this.[1] But his theory of human procreation gave to men alone the role of activating life, while leaving to women the lesser—and more painful—task of carrying that new life to term. Besides being inaccurate, this idea reinforced a patriarchal society's view of males as the dominant and superior sex. Aristotle's theory remained popular well into the Renaissance. Remnants of his and similar concepts still affect thinking today.

Almost 500 years after Aristotle, another Greek philosopher—Galen—developed a somewhat more realistic and egalitarian theory. He believed that the woman, too, produced a seed. But—in true patriarchal style—he was convinced the seed of the male was of greater importance, both in giving spiritual character to the new life and in producing male babies.

Galen and his followers argued against Aristotle's mysogynistic theory, pointing out that females must have an important role in determining the form of offspring; otherwise how could they explain children who looked more like their mothers than their fathers? A Frenchman (whose midwifery book was translated into English in 1672 by Hugh Chamberlen, famed for the invention of forceps) asserted that:

> Asses and mares produce by their coupling mules which are animals of a middle nature resembling both the one and the other that produced them. We may then learn by this that both seeds are necessary for a true conception.[2]

Unfortunately, at this point the philosophers and physicians wandered off on a couple of false tracks. First, they assumed that women produced seeds or sperma in a form of semen, much like men. In fact, many believed the female was an imperfect male, with the same genitalia but inverted within the body instead of forced outside, presumably by the superior warmth of the male. According to this theory, ovaries were internal testicles, and they were even referred to as female testicles.[3]

In a time when magic and miracles often substituted for truth and fact, a fable circulated about a young girl who became very hot from running and took a tremendous leap across a stream, whereupon her genitalia dropped suddenly to the outside of her body, thus causing her to become a man. The idea of inverted organs lingered as late as the nineteenth century, when popular literature still repeated the old saying, "Women are but men turned outside in."[4]

Classical philosophers had another curious idea: males developed in a warm and dry environment, and females formed where it was cold and moist. According to Galen and others, warm and dry conditions would produce a male (like the warm girl who became a boy). Even in our century, a form of contraception—the "rhythm method"—is tied to female temperature as an indicator of fertility.

Despite its scientific errors, Galen's two-seed theory had some redeeming features. His followers in the sixteenth and seventeenth centuries not only gave back to women their rightful role in conception, they also presented women as fully sexual humans who had to enjoy sex, and have an orgasm, in order to produce the seeds—in a female "semen"—to create new life. In other words, both the man and the woman had to eject semen during orgasm, preferably at exactly the same moment.

In some ways this misconception created a more natural sexual environment for both women and men, at least in the seventeenth century, when orgasmic conception was widely accepted as fact. If marriages were meant (as many believed) for the purpose of reproduction, and if new life could only occur as the result of simultaneous orgasm, and if orgasm were a pleasurable condition—then it must follow that men and women ought properly to have healthy sexual appetites. This led to extremes—the picture of the lusty female, hungry for sex, that appeared in caricature and literature throughout this period. But it also created the impression that intercourse was a mutually pleasurable experience, not the rather unwelcome duty of the wife to her husband, as was often believed in later centuries.

Meanwhile, the Judeo-Christian tradition had its own theories and laws on sexuality, most of them restrictive or repressive. These created, over the centuries, the popular notion that sex was, if not evil, at least a deterrent to a proper spiritual life. Virginity and total abstinence were revered in the Roman Catholic church; marriage (and the sexual outlet it provided) was a lesser vocation. Until the Reformation in

England and the abolition of Catholic nunneries, women had a choice between marriage and abstinence. Unfortunately, after the closure of the nunneries, most women were left with few options for a livelihood other than marriage.

Of these ideas, how many filtered down to the woman in the house and the man in the street? The two-seed and orgasmic-conception theories were repeated over and over in the midwifery books and household guides of seventeenth-century England. Of these books, the most popular were Nicholas Culpeper's medical bestsellers that dominated the field in the second half of the seventeenth century. About a dozen editions of his *Directory for Midwives* are known. Other books were translations of European works, such as James Guillemeau's *Child-Birth or, The Happy Deliverie of Women* in the early seventeenth century, and François Mauriceau's *The Accomplisht Midwife* late in the century. John Sadler, like Culpeper an Englishman, wrote *The Sicke Womans Private Looking-Glasse* in 1636. It discussed various uterine ailments on the assumption that women were often too shy to mention such matters to doctors. Unlike Culpeper's books, this one appeared in a single edition.

On the matter of conception, Mauriceau's 1673 midwifery book described it this way:

> The qualifications requisite for a woman to conceive according to nature are that the woman receive and retain in her womb the man's and her own prolific seed without which it cannot come to pass for it is necessary that both seeds should be there. Nor is it at all true, what Aristotle and some other of his followers affirm, that the woman neither hath nor can yield any seed, a great absurdity to believe. For the contrary may easily be discovered, by seeing the spermatic vessels and testicles of a fruitful woman, appointed for this use, which are wholly filled with this seed, which in coition they discharge as well as men.[5]

Culpeper, whose *Directory for Midwives* first appeared in 1651, said, "In the act of copulation the woman spends her seed as well as the man, and both are united to make the conception."[6] He also wrote, "The greater the woman's desire of copulation is, the more subject to conceive she is."[7] (Culpeper was popular in the seventeenth century, though by the late nineteenth century he was decried as a "clever, canting charlatan" by James H. Aveling in his *English Midwives: Their History and Prospects*.)

To be accepted, by this theory, as an equally sexual person also had its drawbacks. The belief in orgasmic conception became one of the most devastating and confusing misconceptions for many unfortunate women. Take, for example, rape. It was a felony, and punishment for it was severe in Elizabethan England. The law supposedly protected women. But a victim of rape was required to report the assault as soon as possible to a responsible person. A single woman could make the complaint herself; if she was married, only her husband could bring action. However, if it was later found that she was pregnant from the rape, she had no case since she presumably enjoyed herself, experienced an orgasm, and thus produced seed to add to the rapist's. Culpeper, who believed that the woman's seed was produced only during orgasm, told his readers, "There never comes conception upon rapes."[8] For the woman, pregnant from a rape, the law was no protection. Confused, bewildered, fearful of public humiliation, such a woman would fail to bring charges. Not surprisingly, few rape cases were recorded in the sixteenth and seventeenth centuries.

Men were not alone in assuming the connection between the woman's seed and orgasm. Jane Sharp—the first female author of a midwifery book (published in 1671) and the only woman publishing in England on the subject between 1475 and 1675—described in frank detail her understanding of the clitoris and its part in conception:

> The clitoris is a sinewy hard body, full of spongey and black matter within it, as it is in the side ligaments of a man's yard [penis], and this clitoris will stand and fall as the yard doth, and makes women lustful and take delight in copulation, and were it not for this they would have no desire nor delight, *nor would they ever conceive.* [Emphasis mine][9]

She repeated the same misconceptions about orgasmic conception that male writers were promoting:

> So by the stirring of the clitoris the imagination causeth the vessels to cast out that seed that lyeth deep in the body.[10]

Mrs. Sharp tried to explain just where the seeds were located:

Below the innermost mouth of the womb they are implanted under the neck of it . . . [and] hold the seed till it is the time of copulation, and then they cast it forth.[11]

Mrs. Sharp also had a theory about monogamy. She explained that even after conception a woman continued to take pleasure in sexual intercourse, making it unnecessary for society to allow polygamy in order to give men an outlet for their sexual urges while their wives were pregnant. (Fornication, adultery, and polygamy were punishable offenses.)

For so soon as a woman conceives, the mouth of the womb is most exactly shut closed, yet they can lie with men all that while, and some women . . . will take more pleasure and are more desirous of their husband's company than before, which is scarce seen in any other female creatures, besides most of them being fully satisfied after they have conceived. *But it was needful for man that it should be so, because polygamy is forbidden by the laws of God.* [Emphasis mine][12]

However, Sadler, writing earlier in the seventeenth century, dissented. He claimed that a woman's "desire to Venus [sexual intercourse] is abated" following conception.[13]

Logic would have suggested that prostitutes who did not become pregnant failed to have an orgasm in spite of what they might have pretended. But this reasoning is hard to find among the male authors—perhaps because men closed their eyes to the possibility that whores might feign pleasure. Instead, an interesting and imaginative explanation appeared in some books:

Other sorts of barren women . . . the whorish crew . . . conceive not, partly by reason that many and various seeds are mingled together, and partly also by reason of their frequent cohabitation with men, whereby the neck of the matrix is made so slippery, that it cannot retain the mans seed.[14]

A number of other problems may have arisen out of the belief in orgasmic conception. Did prostitutes—or even married women who secretly wanted no more children—believe that intercourse without orgasm would protect them from pregnancy? What of the women who pretended orgasm for the sake of their partners and then became pregnant?

Some women, particularly those who experienced many pregnancies, finally may have suspected that much of the advice from scholars and physicians was wrong. They may also have rejected the magic, potions, and suggestions on intercourse positions; and they might have harbored a suspicion they were getting pregnant in midcycle rather than directly after menstruation, the time authors then considered normal. But few women left records that even imply they questioned the folklore or the "experts" who pontificated on such personal matters. Some diaries and journals indicate that marriage could be a terrible burden, or bearing children a cross that could only be borne by constant prayer and religious zeal. But these offer few clues about the sex lives of their seventeenth-century authors.

The population of England was growing during Queen Elizabeth's reign, reaching close to 4 million by the time of her death in 1603. Still, poor public health, plagues, wars, and high infant mortality necessitated a strong birth rate to keep the population robust. Wives of the nobility and wealthy middle class were encouraged to provide heirs; women of lower ranks were expected to produce enough babies to give the family extra hands for the chores of living. Much advice was written on ways to promote pregnancy. Couples might try herbal potions, magic, special intercourse positions, or careful timing within the woman's menstrual cycle. Read the suggestions and take your chances: these two are from Culpeper's bestseller, *A Directory for Midwives*:

> A loadstone [magnet] about the woman causeth not only conception but concord between man and wife. The heart of a male quail carried about the man, and the heart of the female about the woman, furthers conception exceedingly, and causeth mutual love.[15]

Or:

> A plaster of labdanum [gum resin] spread upon leather and applied to the region of the womb, mightily disposeth it to conception.[16]

If you didn't trust salves or amulets, Markham's *English House-wife* suggested:

> To make a woman to conceive, let her either drink mugwort [an herb] steeped in wine or else the powder thereof mixed with wine, as shall please her taste.[17]

Five years later, in *The Sicke Womans Private Looking-Glasse*, there was a suggestion that compares with twentieth-century advice to relax during intercourse in order to conceive:

> Excess in all things is to be avoided. Lay aside all passions of the mind. Shun study and care as adverse to conception.[18]

Today, infertile couples submit to laboratory tests of sperm count and motility, gynecological examinations, and the like. Sixteenth-century couples had fewer tools to work with. *The Byrth of Mankynde*, the earliest printed midwifery book, which appeared in England in 1540, described "how to know whether lack of conception be of the woman or of the man":

> If she take garlic, being pulled out of the husks, and convey of it into the private parts, and if the scent of it ascend up through the body unto the nose, the woman is faultless. If not, then is there lack in her.[19]

There were few tests for deficiency in men other than this garlic test, which in any case was performed on the woman. Culpeper believed women were usually to blame.[20] There was, however, one theory that suggested both partners could be at fault:

> Sometimes the woman proves barren when there is no impediment of either side except only in the manner of the act, as when in the emission of the seed, the man is quick and the woman too slow, whereby there is not a concourse of both seeds at the same instant, as the rules of conception require.[21]

Plenty of other stories told how to test for fertility or how to induce conception. A 1584 book suggested this:

> Take of the ruin of a hare, and having fried and consumed [evaporated] it in hot water, give it the woman to drink in the morning at her breakfast. Then let her stand in a hot bath, and if there come a grief or pain in her belly, she may conceive; if not she shall never conceive.[22]

It might be to the woman's advantage to imagine a "grief or pain," rather than face the suspicion of barrenness. In any case she could fall back on this choice recommendation on how "to make a barren woman bear children," which appeared in the same book:

> Take of these little sea fishes . . . and roast them upon the embers without oil, and let the woman eat of them, and it shall profit and help very much, *having in the meantime the company of a man.* [Emphasis mine][23]

Accurate pregnancy tests were lacking—witness the famous disappointment of Queen Mary's false pregnancy (which turned out to be either edema or a tumor). One primitive test appeared in more than one book:

> Cast a clean needle into the woman's urine put in a brasen [medicine basin], let it stand all night, and in the morning if it be colored with red spots she hath conceived, but if it be black or rusty she hath not.[24]

A few male writers claimed a man could sometimes tell immediately that he had impregnated the woman. In a section titled "Signs to know whether a woman be with child or no," James Guillemeau wrote, in his *Child-birth or, the Happy Deliverie of Women:*

> As for those signs which are taken from the man, they are these: if he find an extraordinary contentment in the company of his wife, and if he feel at the same time a kind of sucking or drawing at the end of his yard; if he return from the field of nature not over-moist, these are signs that a woman may have conceived. And by these observations I have known men *which have assured their wives that they have got them with child, as soon as they have had their company.* [Emphasis mine][25]

Whether such instant knowledge might improve on modern pregnancy and ultrasound tests is an amusing question! Guillemeau conceded, though, that the signs "taken from the woman are more manifest and certain."[26]

The best time in a woman's monthly cycle for conceiving generated great interest and further misconceptions. Late-twentieth-century science believes most ovulation and conception take place about halfway between menstrual periods, but in the seventeenth century writers taught:

> The aptest time for conception is instantly after the months [menstruation] be ceased, because then the womb is thirsty and dry, apt to draw the seed and also to retain it by the roughness of the inward superficies [surface]. And besides, in some the mouth of the womb is turned unto the back or side and is not placed right until the last day of the courses [menstruation].[27]

Or:

> Women are most subject to conceive a day or two after their monthly terms [menstrual periods] are stayed.[28]

Once pregnancy was assured, the next issue was whether the baby would be male or female. In the earliest of printed midwifery books, it was said:

> If it be a male then shall the woman with child be well-colored and light in going, her belly round, bigger toward the right side than the left, for always the man child lyeth in the right side, the woman in the left side.[29]

Guillemeau had these theories:

> They which be with child of a boy are more quick and nimble in all their actions, and be in better health of body, without being subject to many infirmities which commonly happen to women with child of a wench.[30]

Guillemeau's next notion has no sex bias, though the recipe is still suspect:

> An honest gentlewoman assured me that she had made trial of this receipt, which is, to take an equal quantity of claret wine and of urine, made in the morning. Put them together into a glass, and let them stand a whole day. If there appear in the bottom a gross cloud, thick like to bean-broth, it is a sign the woman is with child of a boy. If it appear in the middest [middle], it is sign of a wench. If there be nothing found in the bottom but the ordinary residence of urine, it shows she is not with child at all.[31]

Certain human organs were considered cold and others hot. The result, according to Sadler, was this expectation:

> In the right side of the cavity [womb], by reason of the heat of the liver, males are conceived. In the left side, by the coldness of the spleen, females are begotten. And this do most of our moderns hold for an infallible truth.[32]

Sadler also claimed that "the male is conceived of purer blood and of more perfect seed than the female."[33] However, Culpeper had an idea that must have devastated some men:

> The reason why sometimes a male is conceived, sometimes a female, is the strength of the seed. For if the man's seed be strongest, a male is conceived; if the woman's, a female . . . and that's the reason weakly men get most girls, if they get any children at all.[34]

A girl baby was thought to cause more discomfort for the mother; a boy baby was supposed to quicken sooner. A woman was told to expect red nipples if she were carrying a boy, and black if it were a girl.

But what if a union produced no children? Not everyone thought barrenness was bad. Vives, the Spanish adviser to the first wife of Henry VIII, wrote (and many women might have agreed):

> If thou bear no children, take it with a patient and content mind, and in manner rejoice that thou lackest that incredible pain and business.[35]

On the same subject Sadler's *Sicke Womans Private Looking-glasse*, promised:

> Barrenness maketh women look young, because they are free from those pains and sorrows which other women are accustomed to bring forth withall. Yet they have not that full protection of health which fruitful women do enjoy, because they are not rightly purged of the menstruous blood and superfluous seed, the retaining of which two are the principle cause of most uterine diseases.[36]

Oddly prescient, this warning anticipates recent research that suggests that women who bear late (or never) are at increased risk for breast cancer.

The Roman Catholic church glorified celibacy, and until the Reformation women had the opportunity to live a celibate life in religious orders. Thereafter, when the nunneries were closed and Protestant clergy were permitted to marry and have families, the options for women dwindled. Then the principal role for a female was to marry and bear children—as many as it was her lot to produce. Women like Alice Thornton—who recorded her experiences in a mid-seventeenth-century journal—preferred not to marry but complied with their parents' wishes, only to suffer months, even years, of devastating discomfort from frequent and difficult births.

Sometimes it was important to prevent a pregnancy. Recent scholarship suggests that several methods of contraception were in use in past centuries. Marriage took place relatively late in English common society. In the lower classes marriage was often forbidden until any apprenticeship or service was completed, so marriage—for most—took place in the mid or late twenties. This tended to limit the number of reproductive years for these women.

In the upper classes, where heirs were essential and wealthy young men and women were not apprenticed or required to go into service, this constraint did not apply. As a result of these mores as well as frequent stillbirths, some women found themselves producing babies annually. Only about half of all newborns survived to adulthood.

Menstruation began at a later age, preventing fertility until the young woman was in her midteens. As Culpeper said, "In many the menstruis appear not till after the fourteenth year, in few before, in none till after twelve."[37] Today menstruation can begin by age ten or eleven.

Lower- and middle-class women usually nursed their own babies. This served as a kind of natural contraception; in most women it prevented another pregnancy until the baby was weaned. The result was well-spaced babies, perhaps two years apart. But upper-class women, likely to hire wet nurses, were therefore more prone to frequent pregnancy.

The most reliable contraceptive was complete abstinence. Some people observed a taboo against intercourse while the mother was nursing, believing that, if she became pregnant, the mother's milk would dry up and the nursing baby would starve. One noblewoman wrote that her relatives objected to her nursing a girl baby because it postponed the possible conception and birth of male heirs.[38]

Of course the husband was often impatient to regain his conjugal rights. One nobleman argued:

> It would be a great loss to the Commonwealth in lessening the number of the people, if every mother were obliged to nurse all the children she brings forth, except you think that might be recompensed by the number their husbands would get in other places whilst they are idle.[39]

Sexually active people who could not afford pregnancy used various methods of contraception. According to one recent book, subtitled *Peasants and Illicit Sex in Early Seventeenth-century England,* some couples found satisfaction in mutual masturbation. Others tried coitus interruptus (withdrawing before ejaculation). Some women used sponges, tampons, and douches made of various materials and liquids. The condom, made of oiled animal intestines, was introduced in the late seventeenth century in England. At first it was used primarily as a protection against venereal disease. (Its cost and cumbersomeness prevented widespread use until the invention of vulcanized rubber in the 1840s.)

Still other couples, desperate when these methods failed to prevent pregnancy, resorted to abortion, usually by means of an herbal potion. According to Aristotle, the fetus was not yet animated or "ensouled" until the time of first movement, or "quickening." And although various male authors and church authorities condemned all abortions, self-abortion was quietly practiced as an option until the time of quickening. Severe laws against abortion did not appear until the nineteenth century in England and the United States.

There are no directions for self-abortion in early English guidebooks, but many recipes—under titles such as "How to bring down the courses" or "How to provoke the terms"—gave implicit instructions. These amounted to suggestions on how to bring on menstruation blocked by a pregnancy. While many herbs were proposed, apparently the most effective in terminating pregnancy were savin (related to juniper), pennyroyal, and ergot of rye (a fungus that is still used to contract the uterus). Some of these herbs were poisonous, so even though they did sometimes bring about the desired results, they could also make the woman extremely ill.

Besides using oral abortifacients, women read how to make "pessaries" (a kind of vaginal suppository) to bring on menstruation. These, too, could be interpreted as abortifacients, though how effective they were is questionable. This one was titled a "Pessary to provoke the monthly courses":

> Take the leaves of 2 or 3 handfuls of the herb mercury.[40] Bruise them in a mortar with a pestle, then wrap it in a cloth and bind it fast, and make a pessary the which you shall infuse a little in the juice of the said herb, being warm, and use it.[41]

Menstruation itself was a mystery, and odd beliefs about it abounded. The use of the word "menstruation" was rare in the early midwifery guides. The usual expressions were "courses," "menses," "monthly terms," or "menstruis." Classical writers, who still influenced thinking in the sixteenth and seventeenth centuries, had disagreed on the purpose of menstrual blood. In *A Directory for Midwives,* Nicholas Culpeper tried to summarize the various Greek and Roman theories. He said Hippocrates believed menstrual blood turned to milk in the womb to nourish the fetus. Aristotle, he went on, thought menstrual blood itself nourished the fetus. According to Culpeper, other classical writers denied this, saying menstrual blood was impure and evil:

> because it kills tender herbs, makes trees barren and dogs mad and hurts the women themselves many ways causing pains, swelling, vomiting, loss of appetite, vertigo, the fits of the mother and other sharp and cruel diseases of the womb.[42]

Culpeper himself believed "The child is nourished in the womb by very pure blood."[43] Still, the connection between menstrual blood and mothers' milk (particularly whether one turned into the other), and the good or evil represented by menstrual blood, remained confusing.

When labor commenced, a midwife and invited assistants were sent for. Surprisingly, there were few practical directions for midwives on how to move the unborn child to ease childbirth or how physically to hasten parturition. Yet these would seem to be the most important assistance a midwife could give. Instead there are many concoctions for helping the mother bring forth the baby: herbal medicines, some with labdanum, some with wine or aqua vitae [strong alcohol], all designed to produce a natural childbirth. Culpeper offered three or four simple physical actions for the midwife to take if the baby presented in the wrong position (feet or an arm first or a breech). The midwife was to "reduce it [the baby] into the cavity of the womb when it comes not forth right and place it right," and "labor to put the child in a right posture by moving it with her hand."[44] Culpeper also discussed the use of a caesarian section if all else fails.[45]

Though forceps were introduced by the Chamberlen family of barber-surgeons, they kept their design and use strictly secret; midwives (and even members of the College of Physicians) thus had no chance to work with them for many years. In fact, midwives had little to aid them, other than various potions, oils, and what practical knowledge they had absorbed. One of the potions, "An approved medicine for a woman in labor to make come and prove safe deliverance," from *The Queens Closet Opened*, is of special interest because it mentions specific weights of ingredients. This is rare in Early Modern recipes and remedies:

> Take powder of cinnamon one dram, powder of amber half a dram finely beaten, mingle it with eight spoonfuls of claret wine, and so let her drink it.[46]

(A grain is the smallest English unit of measurement; a scruple is 20 grains or 1/24 ounce; a dram is three scruples or 1/8 ounce.)

Remedies were offered for everything from the "throes" (extreme pain) of childbirth to "puerperal fever" (a serious infection of the uterus that caused death for many mothers) which often followed. Usually remedies involved a drink that eased labor or infection, followed by prayer. Here are two from *The Queens Closet Opened*, the first, "to ease women's childbed throes that are taken with cold a week or two after their delivery":

> Take one or two spoonfuls of oil of sweet almonds newly drawn, either in posset drink or in a caudle warm, morning and evening, it will help.[47]

And the second, "for women's swounding [fainting] fits after delivery of child: "Take the powder of white amber as much as will lie on a three pence, and give it in mace ale warm."[48]

One of many ideas for women having a hard labor was from Markham's *English House-wife*, in which he wrote:

> Take four spoonfuls of another woman's milk and give it the woman to drink in her labor, and she shall be delivered presently.[49]

And to prevent labor and miscarriage, *The Queens Closet Opened* suggested "Dr. Goffes receipt to preserve a woman with child from miscarrying and abortion":

> Take a fillet of beef half roasted hot from the fire, then take half a pint of muscadine, sugar, cinnamon, ginger, cloves, mace, grains of paradise [mezereon, a shrub] and nutmegs, of each half a dram, and make thereof a sauce. Then divide the beef into two pieces and wet them in the sauce, and bind the one piece to the bottom of the woman's belly and the other to the reins of the back, as hot as may be suffered, and keep them on twenty-four hours at the least, and longer if need be thereof.[50]

Culpeper discussed the merits and dangers of purging, or bleeding, a mother who became sick during pregnancy. He decided that "purging is more dangerous than bleeding," and declared:

> You must not give strong purges, lest their force which moveth the humors should reach to the womb and cast out the child. Therefore you must not purge women with child in all diseases, nor at all times, but only in the fourth month till the seventh, and that sparingly.[51]

On the same subject and its relationship to abortion, he protected his profession:

> A Christian may not cause an abortion for any cause, for it is wicked. . . . Nor must the mother be preserved by the loss of the child. . . . But if to preserve the mother, the physician purge or bleed, and the abortion follow, the fault is not in the physician that intended it not, but in the weakness of nature.[52]

108

After childbirth, women might suffer from sore breasts. The breasts of a new mother whose baby was turned over to a wet nurse might be sensitive until the milk dried up. In other mothers the breasts could abscess, causing much pain for a nursing mother, or the abscess could signal a more serious infection. The books offered numerous remedies, while making little distinction between the various problems. This one, from the 1577 *Booke of Sovereigne Approved Medicines and Remedies,* was probably for sensitive skin irritated by the nursing baby:

> Take & temper clean wheat flour with yolks of eggs, and make thereof a plaster & lay thereto, shifting it twice a day, and it will heal the sore.[53]

The Ladies Cabinet Enlarged and Opened provided another "medicine to break and heal sore breasts of woman, used by midwives and other skillful women in London." It was probably for a more serious abscess:

> Boil oatmeal of the smallest you can get and red sage together in running or conduit water till it be thick enough to make a plaster, and then put into it a fit proportion of honey, and letting it boil a little together, take it off the fire, and while it is yet boiling hot, put thereto so much of the best Venice turpentine as will make it thick enough to spread. Then spreading it on some soft leather or a good thick linen cloth, apply it to the breast, and it will first break the sore, and after that, being continued, will also heal it up.[54]

One of Culpeper's cures for inflammation of the breasts was to "open the vein in the ankle and scarify [bleed] the legs, then (if need be) open the arm."[55] He also offered recipes for plasters to ease the pain.

For those women who were not nursing their babies and needed to dry up their milk, *The Ladies Cabinet Enlarged and Opened* offered this prescription:

> Take of oil of linseed and English honey of each a penny worth, white wax half a penny worth, and half a quarter of a pint of sweet butter. Boil all these to a plaster and lay it on the breast.[56]

Once they were no longer lactating, these women were ready to conceive again.

❦

For perspective on these misconceptions, it is useful to go forward to those that evolved in later centuries.

In the eighteenth century, fewer people clung to the two-seed and orgasmic theories of conception, but they were still far from the truth. Speculation on human "preformation," or preexistence, surfaced by the 1700s. Some theorists claimed that tiny miniature people existed in the female egg, and others believed the male spermatozoa contained microscopic humans waiting to be vitalized.[57]

It finally seemed clear that the woman's seed was not released in semen, and that she could conceive without experiencing the pleasure of orgasm. This knowledge percolated through the educated middle class until enlightened society (this was, after all, the Age of Enlightenment) understood that respectable women did not have to be sexually aroused to be fertile, nor indeed were they expected to be lustful to procreate.

What had been seen as active and even passionate participation by women in conceiving babies was reduced to a more passive role, at least among the middle class. This led to mixed signals about women and sex. The upper class might continue to do as it wished. Lower-class women, considered too ignorant to understand, were presumed to continue in their lustful ways. Middle-class women were increasingly seen as passionless and sexually passive, a common (though not always accurate) portrayal in Victorian England. Many of these respectable, and now supposedly asexual, middle-class women must have enjoyed sex while wondering why they did, or if they should. By the nineteenth century, one man—who apparently assumed that female pleasure and passion were unnecessary and even undesirable—wrote, "Complaisance, tranquility, silence and secrecy are necessary for a prolific coition."[58]

An accurate understanding of the mechanics of conception was unknown until the mid-nineteenth century. In 1827 a scientist, Karl Ernst von Baer, identified the ovum in the ovary of a dog. Eventually scientists realized, and more slowly the lay public learned, that the ovum (an egg rather than a seed) is produced on a monthly cycle—and not necessarily at the time of orgasm. Yet to this day we do not fully understand the human reproductive process.

While science is leaping forward in the field of reproduction, no one can claim that present-day knowledge is the final word. We certainly haven't eliminated misconceptions and folklore about conception. But today's understanding of human reproduction is vastly superior to seventeenth-century knowledge. Much of the sense of female inferiority in reproduction, so common in earlier centuries, is gone.

Most women no longer eat certain "little fishes" to try to become pregnant ("having in the meantime the company of a man"). Now the problem is, instead, an exploding population—at a time when most, instead of only half, of all babies survive to adulthood. Meanwhile, in-vitro fertilization, surrogate motherhood, new forms of male and female contraceptives, and safe abortions present difficult ethical questions.

To the men of Early Modern England who wrote the guides and comments on conception, fertility was a prime concern, and they understandably wrote extensively about it. To a society for which infant mortality was a constant threat—when disease, war, and ignorance took most people at an early age—fertility was a vital social issue. But to the women who were "successful" in bearing babies, the knowledge of how to prevent pregnancy may often have been just as important. Today, sufficient knowledge about contraception as well as reproduction is available. However, dissemination of that knowledge is incomplete.

The old misconceptions, put forth in centuries past largely by men and accepted by both sexes, created problems for women. If you were told that female seed was less desirable or potent than male seed, if you were raised with the idea that girls were less perfect than boys, if you thought menstruation was impure or evil, if you believed the woman was to blame when pregnancy resulted from rape, if most advice on how to prevent barrenness was directed toward women on the assumption that they were at fault, if you expected to be in better health while carrying a boy baby—how could all these misconceptions *fail* to instill a belief in female inferiority? And if you had suspicions that some of the "facts" you were taught by the male writers and thinkers were wrong, how would you challenge these errors in a society controlled by writers, scholars, physicians, clerics, and rulers—almost all of whom were men? ❦

Notes

1. For a detailed description see Maryanne Cline Horowitz, "Aristotle and Woman," in *Journal of the History of Biology*, Vol. 9, No. 2 (Fall 1976), 183–213.
2. François Mauriceau, *The Diseases of Women with Child* (1672), 12.
3. See Angus McLaren, *Reproductive Rituals: The Perception of Fertility in England from the Sixteenth to the Nineteenth Century* (London and New York: Methuen, 1984), for detailed descriptions of the procreation theories of Aristotle, Galen, and Hippocrates as well as their cultural and "scientific" interpretations.
4. Thomas Laqueur, "Orgasm, Generation, and the Politics of Reproductive Biology" in *Representations* (Univ. of California Press, Spring 1986), 13.
5. François Mauriceau, *The Accomplisht Midwife* (1673), 12.
6. Nicholas Culpeper, *A Directory for Midwives: or a Guide for Women* (1675), 48.
7. Ibid., 97.
8. Ibid., 70.
9. Jane Sharp, *The Midwives Book* (1671), 43.
10. Ibid., 45.
11. Ibid., 59.
12. Ibid.
13. John Sadler, *The Sicke Womans Private Looking-glasse* (1636), 146.
14. Nicholas Fontanus, *The Womans Doctour* (1652), 133.
15. Culpeper, 97–98.
16. Ibid., 98.
17. Gervase Markham, *The English House-wife* (1631), 40.
18. Sadler, 121.
19. Eucharius Roesslin, *The Byrth of Mankynde* (1540), LXXXIII^v.
20. Culpeper, 73.
21. Sadler, 118–19.
22. John Partridge, *The Treasurie of Commodious Conceits, and Hidden Secrets* (1584), C7^v.
23. Ibid.
24. Sadler, 147.
25. James Guillemeau, *Child-birth or, the Happy Deliverie of Women* (1612), 3–4.
26. Ibid., 4.

27. Sadler, 120–21.
28. Culpeper, 97.
29. Roesslin, LXXXV.
30. Guillemeau, 10.
31. Ibid., 11.
32. Sadler, 7.
33. Ibid., 148.
34. Culpeper, 48–49.
35. Juan Luis Vives, *The Instruction of a Christen Woman* (1529?), fii.
36. Sadler, 112.
37. Culpeper, 75.
38. McLaren, 70.
39. Ibid., 69.
40. Nicholas Culpeper, *Culpeper's Complete Herbal* (Hertfordshire: Omega Books, 1985), 188-90. This reprint of Culpeper's 1653 book describes the plants "French and Dog Mercury," and says, "Hippocrates commended it wonderfully for women's diseases, and applied to the secret parts to ease the pains of the mother; and used the decoction of it to procure women's courses."
41. Philibert Guibert, *The Charitable Physitian with the Charitable Apothecary* (1639), 12.
42. Culpeper, 56.
43. Ibid., 57.
44. Culpeper, Book 4, 180.
45. Ibid., 183.
46. W. M., *The Queens Closet Opened* (1661), 86.
47. Ibid., 118.
48. Ibid.
49. Markham, 39.
50. W. M., 121.
51. Culpeper, Book 4, 160.
52. Ibid., 161.
53. The Booke of Soveraigne Approved Medicines and Remedies (1577), B3.
54. M. B., *The Ladies Cabinet Enlarged and Opened* (1654), 90.
55. Culpeper, Book 4, 206.
56. M. B., 90.
57. McLaren, 22–24.
58. F. E. Fodere, cited in Michael Ryan, *The Philosophy of Marriage* (1837), 331.

Chapter Four

Care of Babies

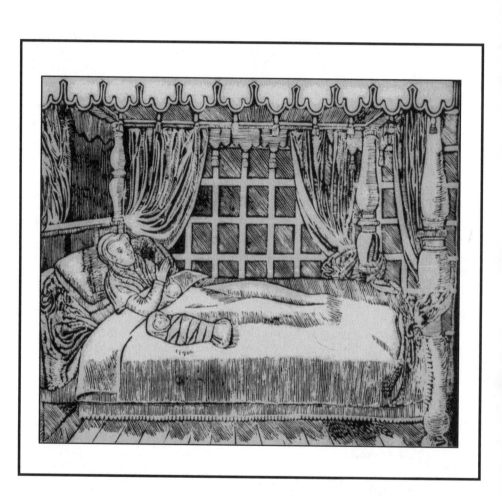

Care of Babies

*A*fter a woman endured the discomforts of pregnancy and the unrelieved torture of childbirth, there was only a fifty-fifty chance her child would survive to adulthood.[1] One quarter of all babies born in Early Modern England died by age ten;[2] many lived only a few hours. The problem affected all levels of society, the upper classes (paradoxically) often more than the lower. (See the chapter on "Rules for Wives.") One famous example was the first wife of Henry VIII, Catherine of Aragon, who bore six children, though only the future Queen Mary lived beyond infancy.

Babies needed breast milk and had trouble surviving if their mothers died. Contemporary records suggest that 1 in 200 women died in childbirth in England;[3] fewer succumbed in New England.[4] Clearly, other perils beyond the death of their mothers carried off newborns and young children.

With death claiming such a large percentage of infants, it would make sense to expect many books advising on their care. This was not the case. Few printed guides to infant care were published; they were usually short appendages to midwifery books. Some books of health remedies mention medicines for children, but few treatises were devoted entirely to their physical care. One exception is Thomas Phaer's 1544 *Boke of Chyldren*.

Opposite page:
MOTHER AND SWADDLED BABY, rubbing of the memorial brass to Anne Savage (1605), St. Katherine's Church, Wormington, Glos. By permission of the Parochial Church Council.

Several factors contributed to this lack. First, most books were written by men, whereas babies were not the hands-on responsibility of fathers. They might regret the loss of a child as much as the mother, though they had little direct experience to pass along. They were, by tradition, excluded from the birthing room; fathers and other men rarely took care of babies.

Second, what knowledge parents and nurses had was passed down through females by word of mouth. Several women were usually invited to attend and help at a birthing. These were not true midwives, but they were expected to be experienced and knowledgeable about the care of newborns.

Third, there was a prevailing assumption that children were small adults, to be dressed and treated as such. Surviving paintings show very young children wearing miniature copies of adult clothing. In practice, of course, a helpless infant could not be treated as a small adult, but rules for a young child's physical care were soon melded into rules for adult care.

Training for religious life was a different story. Plenty of advice was printed on how to lead children to proper Christian living as soon as they were beyond infancy. And there were books of etiquette for children. Two of the earliest books printed in the English language were *The Book of Curtesye,* which told boys how to behave in a noble household, and *The Book of the Knight of the Tower,* a guide for girls. Both books were published in 1484 by William Caxton, the first printer in the English language. But these did not treat on the fundamental physical care of babies and young children.

Another reason few books were published on the proper care of newborns was the widely-held belief that survival or death of any person—baby, child, or adult—was in the hands of God. It did not matter what you did or wished; God's will or mercy determined life or death. It was an age when no real cures or preventatives were known for killer diseases, plagues, and infections. When an individual or even large numbers of children and adults were wiped out, people assumed an all-powerful force was responsible. It was natural to feel helpless with so little scientific knowledge, especially in the matter of fragile babies who had just made the harrowing voyage down the birth canal, and whose survival rate was notoriously poor. A sense of hopelessness in such cases may have contributed to the dearth of practical infant-care books. Mere mortals could do little to save weak infants. How else could Early Modern parents accept the constant loss of new babies? Life or death was God's will.

Several handwritten journals or autobiographies by women, published posthumously, tell of the loss or illness of a child or the recovery of the mother after serious complications of childbirth. The mother invariably writes that the sick or deceased person is in God's hands or subject to the will of the Almighty. Alice Thornton, for example, tells of the births and deaths of six of her nine children. Most died within days of birth, and Mistress Thornton herself often came close to dying. Always she thanked God whether or not the child survived. She writes of her first pregnancy, which ended in miscarriage at about seven months:

> After the miscarriage I fell into a most terrible shaking ague, lasting one quarter of a year, by fits each day twice, in much violence, so that the sweat was great with faintings, being thereby weakened till I could not stand or go. The hair on my head came off, my nails of my fingers and toes came off, my teeth did shake, and ready to come out and grew black. After the ague left me, upon a medicine of London treacle, I fell into the jaundice which vexed me very hardly one full quarter and a half more . . . but still I was upheld by an Almighty Power, therefore will I praise the Lord my God. Amen.[5]

Her fifth child caused her "exquisite torment," and

> the child coming into the world with his feet first caused the child to be almost strangled in the birth, only living about half an hour, so died before we could get a minister to baptize him although he was sent for. And where it was not neglected by us and the means could not be had I trust in the mercies of the Lord for His salvation.[6]

According to a pair of modern demographers, Roger Schofield and E. A. Wrigley, "Most striking is the appalling infant and child mortality."[7] What caused this high rate of infant mortality, besides the whim of some all-powerful being? Difficulty navigating the birth channel, like the Thornton baby, was clearly one reason. Loss of the mother was another.

Deaths also resulted from lack of an antiseptic environment for birthing, difficult and lengthy births, limited or erroneous knowledge by midwives and physicians, and accidents in the handling of the newborn.

Even cultural practices may have caused some deaths. One was the custom—among the upper classes—of farming the baby out to a wet nurse, another mother with enough milk to suckle her own and a second child as well. These surrogate mothers were paid for their services, which may have included housing and caring for the infant. Care was taken in choosing a wet nurse for fear the baby might otherwise adopt the coarse ways of an unsuitable woman. Some reports describe deaths by smothering when the wet nurse had the infant in bed with her. (This must have happened with nursing mothers, too.) Alice Thornton says a wet nurse almost killed one of her early children by falling asleep and rolling on the baby while it was still suckling. When her health permitted, Mistress Thornton breast-fed her babies. This practice was highly recommended in a short treatise, *The Countess of Lincoln's Nurserie* (1622), by Elizabeth Clinton, Countess of Lincoln, the mother of eighteen children. She advised mothers that nursing their own children was a duty they should perform themselves. A generation earlier, Robert Cleaver, in his tome *A Codly [Godly] Form of Householde Governement: For the Ordering of Private Families*, prescribed the same practice:

> Amongst the particular duties that a Christian wife ought to perform in her family, this is one: namely that it belongeth to her to nurse her own children which to omit and to put them forth to nursing is both against the law of nature and also against the will of God. Besides, it is hurtful both for the child's body and also for his wit. And lastly, it is hurtful to the mother herself, and it is an occasion that she falleth into much sickness thereby.[8]

Cleaver also opined:

> The wife is further to remember that God hath given her two breasts, not that she should employ and use them for a show or of ostentation but in the service of God, and to be a help to her husband in suckling the child common to them both. Experience teacheth that God converteth her blood into the milk wherewith the child is nursed in the mother's womb.[9]

Another danger to newborns was swaddling. From birth, babies were wound in cloth to keep them warm and, supposedly, safe. Their arms and legs were bound to their bodies so that they would grow straight. Depending on the weather and the development of the baby, it might live in swaddling clothes for as long as a year. James Guillemeau's "The Nursing of Babies" (bound with his French midwifery book, translated as *Child-birth or, the Happy Deliverie of Women*) was a more extensive and comprehensive child care tract than most. In it Guillemeau, who described himself on the title page of his work as "The French Kings Chirurgion in Ordinary," cautioned:

> We must not only have a regard to such defects of nature as the child may bring with him from his mother's womb, and cure them, but we must also look and have an eye that the nurse or she that swaths and dresseth him do not make him worse.[10]

Men gave nurses and mothers advice on swaddling. The most popular midwifery book from the mid-sixteenth to mid-seventeenth century was Eucharius Roesslin's *Byrth of Mankynde*, translated from Latin into English and published in thirteen editions. The infant-care section of the book warned:

> When the infant is swaddled and laid in cradle, the nurse must give all diligence and heed that she bind every part right . . . and not crookedly and confusely [in a disorderly manner], . . . for in this is it as it is in young and tender imps [shoots], plants and twigs, the which even as ye bow them in their youth, so will they evermore remain unto age. And even so the infant if it be bound and swaddled, the members lying right and straight, then shall it grow straight and upright. If it be crookedly handled it will grow likewise. . . .[11]

Men wanted girl babies to be thought of as future mothers even when they were still in swaddling clothes; thus this warning by Guillemeau in his midwifery book:

> Some swath all the child's body hard to make him have a goodly neck and to make him seem the fatter, but this crushing makes his breast and the ribs which are fastened to the back bone to stand out so that they are bended . . . and that causeth the child to be either

121

crump-shouldered or crooked breasted, or else to have one of his shoulders stand farther out than the other. Some also bind the hips so hard that they become very small, and that hinders them from growing and waxing big, which doth much harm, especially to maids who should have large hips that when they come to age they may bring forth goodly children.[12]

Writers differed on when a baby should be free of swaddling clothes. Guillemeau advised:

About the eighth or ninth month or at farthest when the child is a year old, he must have coats and not be kept swathed any longer.[13]

The first female midwifery writer, Jane Sharp, wrote:

After four months let loose the arms, but still roll the breast and belly and feet to keep out cold air for a year, till the child have gained more strength.[14]

Guillemeau warned nurses "to carry their children sometimes on the right side and sometimes on the left"[15] to prevent bending the knees. No book explains just how to keep a squirming infant quiet enough to bind it up at all. But another French doctor, François Mauriceau, wrote in a 1673 translation of his *Accomplisht Midwife* about the art of swaddling:

It is not necessary to give a particular direction how this ought to be done, because it is so common that there is scarce a woman but knows it, but we'll only say in general that a child must not be swathed too straight. . . . He must be thus swaddled to give his little body a straight figure which is most decent and convenient for a man and "*to accustom him to keep upon the feet, for else he would go upon all four, as most other animals do.* [Emphasis mine][16]

That last phrase sounds as though one of the purposes of swaddling was to prevent crawling.

The baby was wrapped in swaddling clothes soon after birth, but first there were several other rites to observe. Culpeper appended a short section on baby care to his *Directory for Midwives*. In it he said that, immediately after the baby was born, the attending women were to:

Roll it up with soft cloths and lay it in a cradle and wash it first with warm wine; give it a litle honey before it sucks, or a little oil of sweet almonds newly drawn. . .[17]

Guillemeau also had an opinion on "What must be given the child after he is born":

The child being thus shifted and annointed and then well dried and wrapped up by the midwife or others, they must presently give him a little wine and sugar in a spoon, or else the bigness of a pea of mithridate [antidote against poison or infectious disease] or treacle [another remedy or antidote], dissolved in a little wine, if it be winter, and in summer (by reason of the heat) with a little carduus benedictus [blessed thistle] or some other cordial water.[18]

Part of the midwife's duty was to tie the umbilical cord. Roesslin wrote about its later care:

After . . . the part extant or boging forth [protruding] of the navel is fallen, the which commonly chanceth after the third or fourth day, then on the rest remaining strew the powder or ashes of a calf's hoof burned, or of snail shells, or the powder of lead, called red lead, tempered with wine.[19]

And the cord could be put to good use after it fell off. It was part of this recipe from *The Queens Closet Opened* for "A Medicine for a Child that Cannot Hold His or Her Water":

Take the navel string of a child which is ready to fall from him, dry it and beat it to powder, and give it to the patient, child male or female, in two spoonfuls of small beer to drink, fasting in the morning.[20]

Culpeper wrote a mere seven pages on the care of newborns at the end of his *Directory for Midwives*. The first four were guidance in the choice of a wet nurse and the quality of milk the nurse or mother was providing. The few remaining instructions included:

Let it sleep long, carried in the arms often, and give it the dug [nipple], but fill not too much his stomach with milk. . . . The first months let it only suck as often as it will. Give it change of breasts, sometimes the right, sometimes the left. Afterwards make a pap of barley-bread steept in water and boiled in milk. Let strong children have it betimes, and not suck an hour after, thus it must be nourished till it breeds teeth. When the teeth come forth, by degrees give it more solid food, and deny it not milk, such as are easily chewed. When it is stronger, let it not stand too soon, but be held by the nurse or put into a Go-chair that it may thrust forward itself and not fall.[21]

Most of those directions sound familiar today, but not this one: "It is best to wean in the spring or fall, in the increase of the moon, and give but very little wine."[22]

The wrapping and unwrapping of swaddling cloths had to be performed several times a day because the "clout" or "tailclout"—the diaper or nappy—needed to be changed. Guillemeau suggested the following schedule, infrequent by today's standards:

The time of shifting [changing] him is commonly about seven o'clock in the morning, then again at noon, and at seven o'clock at night. And it would not be amiss to change him again about midnight which is not commonly done. But because there is no certain hour, either of the child's sucking or sleeping, therefore divers, after he hath slept a good while do every time shift him lest he should foul and bepiss himself.[23]

Guillemeau even described how the nurse "or some other" should sit while shifting the child:

. . . near the fire, laying out her legs at length, having a soft pillow in her lap, the doors and windows being close shut, and having something about her that may keep the wind from the child. And when she is thus accommodated, she shall unswath and shift him dry. If he be very foul she may wash him with a little water and wine luke warm with a sponge or linen cloth.[24]

There were conflicting suggestions on bathing. This recommendation of Culpeper's is puzzling:

In places where bathing of children is used, let it be washed twice a week from the seventh month till it be weaned.[25]

A century before Culpeper, Roesslin's *Byrth of Mankynde* recommended, on the same subject:

Let it be washed two or three times in the day, and that anon [immediately] after sleep in the winter with hot water, in the summer with luke warm water. Neither let it tary long in the water but unto such time as the body begin to wax red for heat, but take heed that none of the water come into the infant's ear, for that should greatly hurt his hearing another day.[26]

If the baby survived past the first few months, as many did not, there were new problems to be faced, like teething. *The Queens Closet Opened* claimed that this suggestion, "To Make Children's Teeth Come Without Pain," was "proved":

Take the head of a hare boiled or roasted, and with the brains thereof mingle honey and butter, and therewith annoint the child's gum as often as you please.[27]

Mauriceau, the late-seventeenth-century French writer, analyzed several treatments for teething babies and wisely concluded they were based on superstition. Magic and superstition were common substitutes for real knowledge in an age when so few reliable remedies were available.

There are many remedies which divers persons assert have a peculiar property to help the cutting of the teeth, as rubbing them with bitches milk, hares or pigs brains, and hanging a vipers tooth about the neck of the child and other such like trifles; but since they are founded more on superstition than any reason I will not trouble myself to englarge upon what is so useless.[28]

Sadly, small children were susceptible to worms and other internal problems. Treatments, however, might be external, like this one that appeared in *The Closet for Ladies and Gentlewomen* "for children that be so little that the medicine cannot be ministered at the mouth":

You must take very good aqua vitae wherewith you must wash or wet the stomach or breast of the child. Then pour it upon the said place with the powder of fine myrrh, and lay the child down a little while with his breast upward, and you shall see incontinently the worms with the child's dung, come forth dead.[29]

Whether external treatments worked is doubtful. *The Ladies Cabinet Enlarged and Opened* had another recipe for "An Ointment to Kill the Worms in Little Children":

> For stomach worms annoint the stomach with oil of wormwood and the belly with oil of sweet almonds. You must not use any savine in medicines for maiden children but instead of oil of savine take as much of an oxes gall.[30]

Savine was considered an abortifacient, though why it was thought a threat to a small girl is unclear. And here again, almonds—or their oil—are recommended. Almonds were a favorite ingredient in both food and homemade medicines.

The same book had another recipe "For the Worms"; this was an internal treatment: "Drink mares milk as hot as you can have it from the mare, in the morning fasting."[31] And Guillemeau cautioned the child's nurse to "keep a good diet" as a cure for worms:

> Let her abstain from all white meats, raw fruits, peas, beans, fish, and all other meats that are of hard concoction and easy to be corrupted.[32]

Purging was a common remedy for various ills. Guillemeau, again expressing a belief in cures by association, recommended, "If the little one have need to be purged, it will be fitter to give the nurse a purgation than the child."[33]

Smallpox, a dreaded scourge, attacked adults and children alike. Though not always fatal, it threatened the loveliest of complexions with lifelong, unsightly pockmarks in the skin. All three of Alice Thornton's surviving children contracted smallpox. Her lively young daughter, Katherine,

> lost by this sickness her fair hair on her head and that beautiful complexion God had given. The Lord supply her soul with the comeliness of His grace and spirit in her heart, making her lovely in His sight.[34]

But Guillemeau, who wrote extensively on the symptoms and aftermath of smallpox in children, considered disfigurement only one consequence of the disease:

. . . many die thereof, and those which escape do oftentimes bear the marks and badges of this vile disease. I have seen divers children that have been lame and maimed, both of their arms and legs through the very malignity of the humor that fell down upon their tender joints and bones. Others have lost their eyes, or at the least there hath remained some pearl or spot upon them. . . . Some have been deaf. . . . Others have had their nose and mouth shrunk together or else puffed up. . . . The least accident of all is that many have remained disfigured with pits and holes in their faces.[35]

Guillemeau believed smallpox and measles were caused in a child by "the reliques of the menstrual blood wherewith the child hath been nourished" and the "malignity of the air." He recommended fresh air and purges for both the child and its nurse.[36]

Scarred or not, complexions were given special care then, as now. Parents, anxious to assure a fair complexion, could:

Wash the face and body of a sucking child with breast milk or cow milk or mixed with water every night and the child's skin will wax fair and clear and resist sunburning.[37]

Besides beauty, wisdom was a concern of parents. One way to achieve wisdom was this curious suggestion:

Simeon Sethi counselleth women with child to eat many quinces if they desire to have wise children.[38]

Family relationships in the Early Modern period were oddly similar to those of the late-twentieth century, but for a different reason. It was common for a child to have a stepmother or stepfather. Divorce was not the cause of remarriage as it is today; death was. In families where life expectancy was barely half what it is today, mothers and fathers often died before children were out of clouts. This often meant remarriage and a stepparent. New stepparents were cautioned to:

Let the name of step-father and step-mother admonish and put them in mind of their duty towards the children of the one and the other, for step-father and step-mother doth signify a stead-father and a stead-mother, that is, one father or one mother dieth and another succeedeth and cometh in their stead and room. . . . Let the step-mother advisedly consider that God hath ordained and appointed her (in stead of their own mother) to be to them a right true mother, and not only to regard them as children but as orphan children and requireth her to love them and to do them good, as to her own.[39]

The Lisle letters, covering 1533 to 1540, refer to seventeen children and stepchildren of Lord and Lady Lisle, both of whom had been married before and whose first spouses had also had earlier marriages and children. They "were regarded as one family by everybody," and the various children referred to Viscount Lisle as father and signed their letters to Lady Lisle as her sons or daughters, regardless of biological parentage.[40] In any age that would be a lot of children to call one's own.

Despite the dismal level of health care and advice, babies did survive to adulthood, so many that the population of England and its New World plantations burgeoned in the seventeenth century. The writers, of course, had it both ways: every survival stood as a testament to their wisdom, while every death could be excused as the will of God. ❦

Notes

1. Josiah Cox Russell, *British Medieval Population* (Albuquerque: Univ. of New Mexico Press, 1948), 213.
2. Keith Wrightson, *English Society, 1580–1680* (London: Hutchinson, 1982), 105.
3. Roger Thompson, *Women in Stuart England and America* (London and Boston: Routledge & Kegan Paul, 1974), 32.
4. Laura Thatcher Ulrich, *A Midwife's Tale* (New York: Knopf, 1990), 170.
5. Alice Thornton, "Alice Thornton: 1627–1707" in *By a Woman Writt: Literature from Six Centuries by and about Women* (Indianapolis: Bobbs-Merrill, 1973), 43.
6. Alice Thornton, *The Autobiography of Mrs. Alice Thornton*, printed for the Surtees Society (Durham: Andrews & Co., 1875), 95.
7. Roger Schofield and E. A. Wrigley, "Infant and Child Mortality in England" in *Health, Medicine and Mortality in the Sixteenth Century* (Cambridge: Univ. Press, 1979), 139.
8. Robert Cleaver, *A Codly [sic] Form of Householde Governement: For the Ordering of Private Families* (1598), 236.
9. Ibid., 238.
10. James Guillemeau, *Child-birth or, the Happy Deliverie of Women* (1612), 100.
11. Eucharius Roesslin, *The Byrth of Mankynde* (1540), LIIII^v.
12. Guillemeau, 14–15.
13. Ibid., 23.
14. Jane Sharp, *The Midwives Book* (1671), 374.
15. Guillemeau, 15.
16. François Mauriceau, *The Accomplisht Midwife* (1673), 363.
17. Nicholas Culpeper, "A Tractate of the Cure of Infants" in *A Directory for Midwives* (1675), 229.
18. Guillemeau, 22.
19. Roesslin, LIIII^v.
20. W. M., *The Queens Closet Opened* (1661), 91.
21. Culpeper, 230.
22. Ibid., 231.
23. Guillemeau, 21.
24. Ibid.
25. Culpeper, 230.

26. Roesslin, LV.
27. W. M. , 47.
28. Mauriceau, 403.
29. *A Closet for Ladies and Gentlewomen* (1611), 145.
30. M. B., *The Ladies Cabinet Enlarged and Opened* (1654), 82.
31. Ibid., 83.
32. Guillemeau, 55.
33. Ibid., 62.
34. Thornton (1875 ed.), 157.
35. Guillemeau, 110.
36. Ibid., 111.
37. Hugh Platt, *Delightes for Ladies* (1603), G10^v.
38. Henry Buttes, *Dyets Dry Dinner* (1599), C6.
39. Cleaver, 240.
40. *The Lisle Letters, An Abridgement*, ed. Muriel St. Clare Byrne (Chicago: Univ. of Chicago Press, 1983), 86.

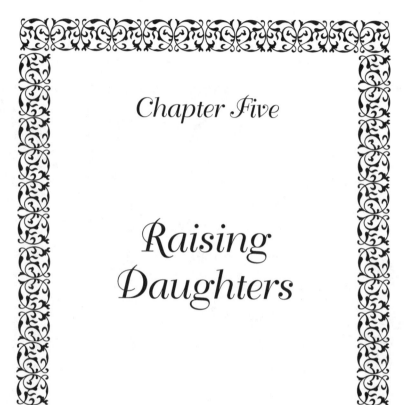

Chapter Five

Raising
Daughters

Raising Daughters

*D*aughters could be serious disappointments. Not always, of course, but in a culture that bequeathed wealth and property through a system of primogeniture, it was important to have male heirs. Even in the laboring classes they were more desirable; a male worker commanded a higher wage than a female for the same work. The Lisle family letters of the sixteenth century include a comment, after a daughter's birth, that "by God's grace at the next shot she [the mother] shall hit the mark."[1]

Although prescriptions for raising daughters in middle- and upper-class families differed largely from those for raising sons, there were two major exceptions. Both girls and boys were taught the basic tenets of Christianity at an early age. And both were expected to learn to respect and obey their parents. Thomas Becon, who wrote a massive two-volume how-to-live guide early in Queen Elizabeth's reign, advised parents:

> So soon as the children be able to speak plainly, let them even from their cradles be taught to utter not vain, foolish, and wanton, but grave, sober, and godly words; as, God, Jesus Christ, faith, love, hope, patience, goodness, peace, etc. And when they be able to pronounce whole sentences, let the parents teach their children such sentences as may kindle in them a love toward virtue, and an hatred against vice and

sin; as for an ensample: God alone saveth me. Christ by his death hath redeemed me. The Holy Ghost sanctifieth me. There is one God . . .[2]

Half a century later the anonymous author of *The Office of Christian Parents* advised:

First, therefore let the parents teach these young infants the Lords Prayer . . . and it being perfect, then the creed, and after it . . . the ten commandments.[3]

Alice Thornton begins her autobiography by saying that her "dear and pious" parents instilled

. . . my strict education in the true faith of the Lord Jesus Christ [and] the principles of grace and religion . . . with my milk . . .[4]

As they grew older, children of both sexes were drilled in the questions and answers of the catechism. Becon uses the catechismal method to present his ideas of family governance and obedience to parents. A son gives lengthy responses to a father's comments and questions about family relationships. For example, the son, making a rote remark, says, "The office and duty of children toward their parents consisteth in two things," and the father asks, "What two things are they?" The son replies:

Honor and obedience. That child which will do his office truly and faithfully, according to the commandment of God, must both honor and obey his father and mother.[5]

Note that the dialog is between a father and son. There are sections pertaining to daughters, wives, and widows, but any conversation is always between the father and son. The son is taught how to govern the women in his life. True to contemporary tradition, the females are silent.[6]

Becon takes only one page of dialog to cover "The Office and Duty of Young Men Unmarried." Their major missions are to honor and heed their elders, to occupy themselves with honest and lawful pastimes, to avoid idleness and evil company, and to keep their bodies "unpolluted," so that their offspring will be clean and strong.

But it takes almost five times as long to cover the proper behavior and "Duty of Maids and Young Unmarried Women." Girls must, according to Becon, pray for help in remaining pure and chaste; they must obey masters and mistresses and carry out their commandments faithfully; they must avoid "running about" with company that indulges in "singing, dancing, leaping, skipping, playing, kissing, whoring, etc";[7] they must dress themselves modestly, sequestering their minds "from the filthy desires of vain and light apparel."[8] They must:

> be not full of tongue, and of much babbling, nor use many words, but as few as they may. . . . For there is nothing that doth so much commend, avance, set forth, adorn, deck, trim, and garnish a maid, as silence.[9]

The properly raised daughter had not only *prescriptions* for behavior but *restrictions* on her activities much beyond those suggested for her brothers. One chapter of *The Court of Good Counsell,* an early-seventeenth-century guidebook, was called "Of the diversity of the care that parents ought to take of their daughters in bringing up of them more than they take for the bringing up of their sons." It, like Becon's rules, claimed "that the father is to use himself otherwise toward them [daughters] than toward his sons."[10]

The daughter was also to "use herself otherwise," to borrow the phrase, toward her father than toward her mother. She was to obey her parents; that was one of the two earliest lessons. But she must always remember that her father is the head of the family. If problems arose, the father's word was supreme—particularly when the father was a king. A letter from an imperial ambassador described the insistence of Henry VIII that his daughter, Mary Tudor, obey him—not her mother, Queen Catherine of Aragon—and concluded:

> . . . although sons and daughters were bound to some obedience towards their mothers, their chief duty was to their fathers, and [the princess] must submit to his pleasure.[11]

The books agreed that it was the father's responsibility to settle his daughter in an appropriate marriage and to see that she was brought up as a chaste and worthy candidate for that goal. But the father was cautioned to consider the class in which his daughter would be a wife.

Class was the key to daughter-raising, as it was to most of life. Acceptable accomplishments for marriage into one class were often quite different from those of another. *The Court of Good Counsell* advised:

> It behooveth then all discreet fathers, who are to bestow their daughters in marriage, to consider of what calling his son-in-law is like to be, and so to frame his daughter accordingly: as, if he purpose to marry her into the country, to bring her up in country housewifery. If the father mean to marry his daughter to a courtier, he must let her to the court to the service of some great lady, and must be learned to read, to write, to discourse, to sing, to play on instruments, to dance, and to be able to perform all that, which belongeth to a courtier to do: by this means many are married to great gentlemen, without one penny dowry given by their father.[12]

(Presumably the young woman who could marry into court circles without a dowry was not only well prepared but also physically attractive.)

Generally, the class a girl was born into defined her education. Or—put differently—the class a girl was expected to marry into defined her education. Middle-class, gentry, and aristocratic daughters were all raised to become wives. But a wife's duties—and the training required—could vary. As the last quotation suggests, in the upper classes the accent was placed not entirely on household skills but also on polished accomplishments—the ability (and wherewithal) to dress elaborately, to dance well, to play an instrument, perhaps to perform in private masques. Politesse and skill in conversing and dressing with style and panache were considered requirements at court. As Castiglione argued in his *Courtier*, translated into English in 1561,

> principally in her fashions, manners, words, gestures and conversation (me think) the woman ought to be much unlike the man. . . . that in going, standing, and speaking what ever she lusteth may always make her appear a woman without any likeness of man. . . . For many virtues of the mind I reckon be as necessary for a woman as for a man. Likewise nobleness of birth, avoiding affectation or curiosity, to have a good grace of nature in all her doings, to be of good condition, wit, foreseeing, not haughty, not envious, not ill tongued, not light, not contentious, not untowardly . . .

Castiglione, of course, was writing of the sophisticated Italian courts. Unlike many writers who taught only silence for a woman, he commends a woman's ability to converse well with men but admitted:

> Me think well beauty is more necessary in her than in the courtier, for (to say the truth) there is a great lack in the woman that wanteth beauty.[13]

But he writes about a lady courtier. Daughters of tradesmen, city merchants, well-to-do yeomen, and even country gentry were warned to avoid the skills and clothes considered appropriate for upper-class girls, and concentrate instead on housewifely tasks.

Guidebooks published in the seventeenth century assumed that the classes they addressed could read and write. Yet among the literate of the middle and upper classes there were clear differences of opportunity based on sex. Much has been written about such women as Lady Jane Grey, Thomas More's daughters, and Queen Elizabeth who, in the early 1500s, were students of Latin and Greek. These ladies were extremely rare. Tales of their abilities may give the impression that a classical education for women was encouraged, admired, and generally available. It was not. These ladies received private tutoring—by men—in their homes. But tolerance for female education in classical languages was limited. It became even less common in the seventeenth century as strife between Roman Catholics and Protestants identified Latin as the language of the outlawed Catholics.

For those of the "middling sort," reading and writing skills were acceptable. William Gouge, in his *Of Domesticall Duties,* wrote:

> Children are to be trained up in those things which are the groundwork of all callings, as reading, writing and principles of learning. Whatsoever the particular calling be, these will be of great use to anyone.[14]

A classical education for daughters, however, did not meet with approval. Lady Grace Mildmay's journal reveals that she and her sisters were educated at home by a cousin under the supervision of their mother. They were taught basic reading, writing, and arithmetic, as well as deportment, religious concepts, and domestic skills. The latter included studies in surgery, pharmaceuticals, and needlework.[15] Alice Thornton wrote that she was fortunate to receive her education (while her father was stationed in Ireland) along with two young ladies,

> learning those qualities with them which my father ordered, namely, the French language, to write and speak the same; singing, dancing, playing on the lute and theorbo [a type of large lute with double neck]; learning such other accomplishments of working silks, gumwork, sweetmeats, and other suitable houswifery, as by my mother's virtuous provision and care, she brought me up in what was fit for her qualities and my father's child. But above all things, I accounted it my chiefest happiness wherein I was trained in those pious, holy, and religious instructions, examples, admonitions, teachings, reproofs, and godly education, tending to the welfare and eternal happiness and salvation of my poor soul, which I received from both my honored father and mother, with the examples of their chaste and sober, wise and prudent conversations in all things of this world.[16]

Sir Ralph Verney, many of whose letters have survived, was clearly opposed to classical learning for girls. He wrote, regarding his own daughter:

> Pegg is very backward. . . . I doubt not but she will be scholar enough for a woman. . . . Let not your girl learn Latin, nor short hand; the difficulty of the first may keep her from that vice, for so I must esteem it in a woman.[17]

To his goddaughter he wrote:

> I did not think you had been guilty of so much learning as I see you are . . . believe me a Bible (with ye Common Prayer) and a good plain catechism in your mother tongue being well read and practised is well worth all the rest and much more suitable to your sex . . .[18]

Sir Ralph favored proficiency in the French language,

> for that language affords many admirable books fit for you, as romances, plays, poetry, stories of illustrious (not learned) women, receipts for preserving, making creams and all sorts of cookeries, ordering your gardens and, in brief, all manner of good housewifery. If you please to have a little patience with yourself (without Hebrew, Greek, or Latin)

when I go to Paris again I will send you half a dozen of the French books to begin your library.[19]

Clearly, he approved the reading of French romances. Light literature did not seem to bother him despite the fact that he was writing during the period of the Commonwealth. In those years of the ascendancy of Puritan culture, even the theatres were closed.

A much stricter approach to reading was promoted a century earlier. At that time Thomas Salter called reading by young girls of "heart books, ballads, songs, sonnets and ditties of dalliance" a "pestilent infection," and said such writing ought to be forbidden to a maiden, since they might "make her mind (being of itself very delicate) more feeble and effeminate."[20] No gifts of romances from him. No music, either. Salter's *Mirrhor of Modestie* [1579] was a translation from the Italian. The original, by Giovanni Bruto, had certain similarities to emerging Puritan ideas. Bruto, like Verney, was strongly against learning for girls:

> Let the small profit got by learning be compared with the great hurt that may happen unto them, and they shall be shown (if nevertheless they remain opinious therein) how much more convenient the needle, the wheel, the distaff, and the spindle, with the name and reputation of grave and honest matrons is for them than the book and pen with an uncertain report if in them there be more learning than honestie & virtue.[21]

The book was later published (1598) in a three-language version—English, Italian, and French—as *The Necessarie, Fit, and Convenient Education of a Yong Gentlewoman*. However, neither was very popular, warranting only one edition apiece.

Even the most restrictive guidelines for females did not entirely rule out reading—provided, as some said, that there was careful oversight of the subject matter. Journals and letters written by women suggest that they were reading a broad spectrum of books; after 1570 a growing number of books, including romances, were addressed specifically to a female audience. Women's letters and journals tell of reading (or hearing) a variety of writing, from solemn sermons to Turkish travel books to the most censored of romances like *Amadis of Gaul*. Among the romance-readers were Anne Clifford, Countess of Dorset, Pembroke, and

Mongomery; Elizabeth Pepys, the wife of Samuel Pepys, the diarist; and Dorothy Osborne, who wrote dozens of chatty letters to her future husband, Sir William Temple. Sir Philip Sidney's *Arcadia*, as well as John Lyly's best-selling *Euphues* series, sought out female audiences. French romances, published as lengthy serials, were popular in the original language as well as in translation. These types of books went into multiple editions, suggesting that women were, in fact, enjoying them. The harsh restrictions, then, of the most conservative male writers were ignored among parts of the literate population.

The popular and massive *Book of Martyrs*, whose official title was *Actes and Monuments*, found a place in many homes despite its size. According to Lady Grace Mildmay, *Martyrs* provided her with helpful female role models.[22] Controversial essays on a woman's place in society, directives for a virtuous female life, and practical household guidebooks all sought a female audience. The most conservative women, however, admitted only reading the Bible, other religious material, and perhaps an herbal. Margaret Hoby and Alice Thornton fall in this group. Bishop Lewis Bayly, in his well-known *Practise of Pietie*, wrote a section called "How to read the Bible with profit and ease once over every year." If his advice were followed by the conscientious, it would use up a great many reading hours.

For some, lessons in writing accompanied lessons in reading, though many learned only to write their own names. An example is described by Muriel St. Clare Burne, the editor of *The Lisle Letters,* which date from the 1530s. She mentions a daughter each of Lord Lisle and his wife—offspring of earlier marriages. The girls, Philippa and Frances, were both in their late teens, and

> ... the only accomplishment of which they give evidence is needlework. Francis may have been able to write, but there are no letters from Philippa. She could apparently read . . .[23]

Another daughter of Lady Lisle, Anne Basset—who was briefly a maid of honor to Jane Seymour, third wife of Henry VIII—dictated a letter to her mother. The last paragraph read:

And whereas ye do write to me that I do not write with my own hand, the truth is, that I cannot write nothing myself but mine own name, and, as for that, when I had haste to go up to the Queen's chamber, my man did write it which did write my letter.[24]

In the early part of this period an upper-class girl or boy was often "placed out" to serve in the home of a prominent family friend or relative, and there he or she received practical instruction in polite conduct—so important in the upper ranks of society. The Lisle family in the 1530s was headquartered in Calais, France, where Lord Lisle (the illegitimate son of King Edward IV) was King's Deputy, or Governor. The vast collection of their letters reveals that they were much concerned with the placing of two young daughters of Lady Lisle's earlier marriage.[25] Ultimately the girls served in prominent French households for several years. Their training (and beauty) then opened important doors for them at the English court—Anne, the one who admitted she could only write her own name, to Jane Seymour's retinue; the other to service with another noble lady. Beauty, manners, and the proper connections were vital to such appointments. Apparently, the ability to write was not.

On the other hand, editor Byrne notes that another sister, Mary, could and did write in her own hand. These girls were aristocrats, and one was the granddaughter of a king; all were descendants of noble families. They were, clearly, not all educated alike. It must be remembered that in well-to-do families both men and women dictated to secretaries in much the same way that business correspondence is handled today. They probably could read, though they did not need to be able to write.

Almost a century later Martin Billingsley produced a penmanship book in which he touted writing for women, though with limitations. His reasoning was interesting. Private communication between man and wife, or friend and friend, he said, would be improved if all had writing skills, and:

The practice of this art is so necessary for women, and consequently so excellent, that no woman surviving her husband, and who hath an estate left her, ought to be without the use thereof . . .

She would then not need to trust

to the reports of such as are usually employed to look into the same: whereas otherwise for want of it, she is subject to the manifold deceits now used in the world, and by that means plungeth herself into a multitude of inconveniences.[26]

In other words, good old English practicality entered the picture. A woman could better handle business operations in her husband's absence if she could read and write without depending on the honesty of her aides. And correspondence by middle-class women who had no secretaries, but were literate, likewise became more important.

So, reading and sometimes writing were acceptable skills for daughters, but only in those classes or families where they were considered useful and suitable. This excluded masses of women in laboring families, where there were neither books nor readers, and where any necessary documents were signed with an X or similar "signature."

Girls learned to read and write in a number of places—at home with a tutor, at another home, at the petty (elementary) schools (if one were nearby where both boys and girls could learn basic use of the English language), and, by the seventeenth century, in girls' boarding schools.[27] Boarding schools gradually took the place of both the outlawed nunnery (Roman Catholic) schools and the tradition of placing out in other homes. They cost more than most families could afford. Some, though, were founded as a kind of apprenticeship for orphans or poor girls, where they probably learned to read. More important to the school sponsors, they learned a marketable skill, such as weaving or lace-making.

Until well into the seventeenth century, when private boarding schools became more common, most girls of the middling sort received their education at home or in another home where they were placed out to serve and learn. Besides reading and writing, such daughters learned to run a household, sew, create fine needlework, and, in some families, speak a foreign language. This was usually French, almost never Latin or Greek. The classical languages were for men, and the grammar schools and universities where they were taught were forbidden to females.

But what of the laborers, the poor husbandmen, those who lived a hand-to-mouth existence, owned no land, and could ill afford even the necessities of life. How were their daughters raised? The largest numbers of families—the lower classes—left almost no personal written records. They were, as a rule, uneducated and unable to record their lives in written form. Literature and contemporary drama offer few clues. They often cast the poor and uneducated as servants or buffoons, while offering little insight into their home lives.

Ballads—and the cartoon-like illustrations that accompanied printed versions of these "street songs"—give a somewhat more realistic picture. Occasionally they tell a tale of the daughter of a poor family who, through her beauty or evil actions, becomes notorious. The song of the "Blind Beggar's Daughter of Bednal Green"[28] is an example. The beggar's lovely daughter found many wealthy and titled suitors in a nearby town, but as soon as they learned her father was a beggar they backed off until it was discovered the beggar had wealth and a heroic past. According to the ballad, beauty alone could not overcome class without strong compensations (usually financial). On the other hand, there were also warnings against marrying daughters to tradesmen for their wealth instead of to poorer, younger sons of a "fine" family:

> For men will sooner match their daughters with my yong maister, a rich coblers sonne, though they be their heires, then with a gentleman of good house, being a yonger brother. Heerby comes the decay of ancient gentilitie, and this the making of upstart houses.[29]

In the poorest families it would be more realistic to say that children of either sex were raised for labor. At an early age both boys and girls from poor homes were given tasks that might contribute to the family's subsistence. In the country, where most of the population lived, this might mean caring for any family animals or taking cattle and sheep to the commons or helping with any of the parents' labors—whatever could bring in a small coin or otherwise supplement the hand-to-mouth existence. Even so, some division of training took place, with boys imitating fathers and girls learning household tasks from their mothers. Boys and girls, living in the country, were expected to perform hard physical work as well.

Formal education—everything from basic reading and writing through university study and foreign travel—was not an option for most people of either sex. Early in the seventeenth century it was still rare to find country women who could sign their own names.[30] Laboring families were in most cases precluded from attending schools, as even the pittance charged by schoolmasters was beyond their means. Also, in the lower classes reading and writing were rarely thought important. A family had to want book learning and had to instill that desire in their children. Few found reading and writing skills valuable enough to commit money and time to them.

Beyond reading, writing, and possibly a marketable skill, daughters were expected to learn housewifery as preparation for marriage. This training, too, could be acquired in various places. An upper-class girl was taught how to supervise a large staff; instruction was given in her home, or when she was "placed out" to another home. For girls of lower classes home management could be learned from a different angle if the daughter were committed at an early age as a servant. This was different from placing out. It was, instead, similar to apprenticeships for young boys, who were contracted for a number of years to learn a craft. Apprenticeship and service postponed marriage for young men and women until their commitments were completed, usually in their late twenties. For most girls, the basics—cooking, brewing, distilling, sewing, care of children as well as small animals and birds, and the countless minutiae that made up family living—were taught from early childhood. In the country homes of husbandmen, yeomen, and gentry families these lessons were taught by the mother or another adult female. Similar training was also found in urban families, especially those of tradesmen and professionals. After all, town and country were not as far apart as they are today. The largest city, London, though growing rapidly, still had only about 200,000 residents by 1600.

Deportment, proper behavior, and manners were also core subjects for both middle-class and aristocratic daughters. Manners were vital to the upbringing of either upper-class daughters or daughters of middle-class families with dreams of social advancement. In the early part of this period Erasmus wrote *A Lytell Booke of Good Maners for Chyldren*. The book was published in two columns, one in Latin, the other in "the vulgare Englysshe." It got right down to basics, describing the proper manner of blowing the nose, warning not to cough in another's face nor to walk up and down the aisle in a church when a service was in progress, and telling how to spit without spraying others. Erasmus was probably directing his instructions to boy "chyldren," but some etiquette rules could be used by girls as well. For example:

> To lick thy fingers greasy or to dry them upon thy clothes be both unmannerly. That must rather be done upon the board cloth or thy napkin. To swallow thy meat hole down is the manner of storks and devouring gluttons. . . . To peal thy eggshell with thy fingers or thy thumb is a leud touch: the same is more leud to put thy tongue in to the egg. With thy knyfe to take it out is more comely. . . . To gnaw bones is the property of dogs. To pick it with thy knife is good manner. To take salt out of the salt cellar with three fingers in a vulgar jest is called the norter [nurture, custom] of carters and ploughmen. Salt must be taken as is necessary with thy knife. If the salt be far off it must be asked. To lick the dish wherein is sugar or any sweet meat is the property of cats and not of men.[31]

Fathers of girls of the middling sort were particularly cautioned in the proper upbringing of their daughters. An insistence on chastity, silence, meekness, modesty, and obedience permeated the literature. Fathers were expected to be vigilant gatekeepers, allowing no attempts on their unsullied daughters until the day of marriage.

Marriage, of course, was the goal of all this training and control, the "graduation" from the school of housewifely training and the entry into its practical application. Male-authored books offered plenty of opinions on the proper way to find an acceptable marriage partner. The advice was aimed largely at middle- or upper-class families. In the noble and affluent classes, marriage was a form of business contract that united lands and other sources of wealth. Arranged marriages were common, as is clear from Lady Brackwell's famous dictum: "When you do get engaged to anyone, I or your father, should his health permit, will inform you of the fact."[32] This quote also suggests the important role mothers took in arranging marriages. It was the father's responsibility to see his daughter suitably married, while the mother often handled much of the scouting and negotiating. Young people were expected to accept unions arranged by their parents. After all, they were brought up to be obedient. But, according to Becon, no matter how advantageous an arranged marriage appeared to be, ideally neither the man nor the woman was to be forced into an unwelcome marriage:

> The authority of the parents be great over their children, yet in the matter of marriage the consent of the children may not be neglected . . . that the authority of the parents and the consent of the children may go together, and make perfect an holy and blessed marriage.[33]

Neither were two people to undertake marriage without the consent of parents or guardians. Unfortunately, arranged marriages (and in some cases love matches) resulted in much unhappiness, divisiveness, and legal wrangling over property. Wives' portions and personal property fell under the control of their husbands, who were not always generous in sharing that wealth once they controlled it.

Young girls were taught, marital problems or no, to learn to love their husbands. This did not mean learning to lust after him. In fact, girls approaching sexual maturity (this occurred later in past centuries, about age fourteen) were cautioned to suppress "carnal lust" by eating and drinking modestly until they were mature enough for marriage and the production of strong babies. To love one's spouse was a Biblical commandment. The wife was expected to love, honor, and respect (and sexually tolerate) her husband, as well as to produce babies and keep a good house. The husband, too, was entreated to love his wife, though the onus on the woman seemed much stronger. Wedding vows reinforced this commandment. The 1559 *Book of Common Prayer* asked the woman if she would:

> have this man to thy wedded husband, to live together after God's ordinance in the holy estate of matrimony? Wilt thou obey him, and serve him, love, honor, and keep him, in sickness and in health? And forsaking all others, keep thee only to him so long as you both shall live?[34]

(Note that, to this day—nearly four and a half centuries later—much the same oath is administered in traditional Christian weddings.) Further along in the ceremony the bride is again required "to love, cherish and to obey." The man vowed only to love, comfort, honor, and keep his wife.

At least one writer was cynical about those vows, however. Speaking of the wife, Thomas Carter wrote, ". . . it will appear (as I said) for the most part that they never regard that vow."[35] He was not only a pessimist; he was strict and severe. Regarding a son, he recommended that the father "beat him on the sides while he is a child if disobedient," and, in dealing with a daughter, "show not thy face cheerful towards them. Marry thy daughter and so shalt thou perform a weighty matter."[36]

By the time girls reached marriageable age they were often the majority sex. And what of the girls who never found a partner or whose parents failed in this duty? Being an "old maid' was not an enviable position, though surviving letters and journals suggest that some women might have preferred a single life and no childbirth. But most young women seemed to expect marriage and feared remaining single. Some of the verses of "The Wooing Maid," a ballad by Martin Parker—one of the most popular of the balladers—tell the sad story of the woman who could not find a man:

> I am a fair maid, if my glass do not flatter,
> Yet by the effects I can find no such matter,
> For everyone else can have suiters great plenty,
> Most marry at fourteen, but I am past twenty,
>
> (*Chorus:*)
> Come gentle, come simple, come foolish, come witty,
> Oh, if you lack a maid, take me for pity.
> I see by experience—which makes me to wonder—
> That many have sweethearts at fifteen and under,
> And if they pass sixteen, they think their time wasted.
> O what shall become of me? I am out-casted.
>
> Whoever he be that will ease my affliction,
> And cast upon me an auspicious affection,
> Shall find me [so] tractable still to content him,
> That he of his bargain shall never repent him.
> (*Chorus*)
>
> I'll neither be given to scold nor be jealous.
> He ner shall want money to drink with good fellows.

147

While he spends abroad, I at home will be saving.
Now judge, am not I a lass well worth the having.
(*Chorus*)

Let none be offended, nor say I'm uncivil,
For I needs must have one, be he good or evil.
Nay, rather than fail I'll have a tinker or boomman,
A pedlar, an inkman, a matman, or some man.[37]

This ballad has a certain tongue-in-cheek element to it (as, of course, do many ballads). It is hardly a true picture of any but the upper classes, where young people were married off at a young age to bear heirs. The lower classes were constrained from the early marriages by apprenticeship and service, which delayed marriage until well over fourteen. Still, it is a classic image of the fear of spinsterhood.

An unmarried woman remained in the care of her father or, upon his death, his heir. She was often dependent on relatives for her home, her allowance, her very living. Or, lacking appropriate relatives, she might become the ward of another man, who then had the right to control her inheritance (if any) and to marry her off as he wished. Such a woman had little status, often little money, and an uncertain future. Writers gave consideration to this situation, particularly in regard to daughters in lower or middling society. Becon advised that these girls should be taught

> to give themselves to honest and virtuous exercises, to spinning, to carding, to weaving, to sewing, to washing, to wringing, to sweeping, to scouring, to brewing, to baking, and to all kind of labors without exception, that become maids of their location, of whatsoever degree they be, rich or poor, noble or unnoble, fair or foul. This thing shall help greatly in time to come to get their living, if need require.[38]

This is a telling prescription. Females are to stay at home and handle a vast number of household chores, but if "need require"—that is, if they have to earn a living—they may use these distaff skills to support themselves. Marriage and housekeeping activities were the acceptable vocation for females—the role they were raised to follow in middle- and upper-class families. Yet a woman of almost any class might be forced to make a living outside her family duties. If so, acceptable commercial activities might include making and selling food and drink, weaving, sewing, and serving—all tied in some way to the home and domestic duties.

Some middle-class fathers prescribed "counting" as an acceptable vocation in a time of need and requested that such training be part of their daughters' education. The Verney letters relate the worries of a relative (a doctor) who had a daughter whom he wanted to place out with the Verneys. (They were reluctant.) The doctor wanted the girl trained in reading, writing, dancing, singing, guitar-playing, speaking French, and "as many trades as I could to get her living by, for I am in no great likelihood to provide her a portion." He especially wanted her to learn "to write and cast account."[39]

The literature is quite clear that fathers had the final responsibility for seeing that their daughters were raised in an appropriate fashion. But it is also evident that mothers, or other women, carried out most of the day-to-day education. They had hands-on charge of sons until they reached age seven, at which time boys in more advantaged homes would enter into more formal education, often away from the home. By contrast, daughters were under female tutelage until maturity. More than one male writer pointed out that girls might be improved by an education like their brothers', but most seemed to think that:

> Men have their parts cultivated and improved by education. . . . And truly had women the same advantage [as men], I dare not say but they would make as good returns of it. . . . And were we sure they would have . . . humility enough to poise them against the vanity of learning, I see not why they might not more frequently be intrusted with it. . . . But . . . let it be admitted that in respect of their intellects they are below men.[40]

In other words, the assumption was that females had lesser intellects and could not always be trusted to use knowledge wisely, though it probably would not hurt society or the girls if they were to get more education—rather tepid support, indeed. Subsequently, various writers conceded that women are equal in one way with men: they both have God-given souls.

Richard Mulcaster, the best known of sixteenth-century schoolmasters, favored a somewhat limited reading and writing education for young girls. But he emphasized boys' education, "because naturally the male is more worthy and politically he is more employed."[41]

A short and popular guidebook was Thomas Powell's *Tom of All Trades, Or the Plaine Path-way to Preferment*. It espoused the Puritan line—no dancing, no foreign-language instruction, no exaggerated fashions for daughters. For the sons, however, Powell ordered fathers to

> be sure that they all have grammar [Latin] learning at the least. So shall they be able to receive and retain the impression of any the said professions. And otherwise shall scarce possibly become masters in the same, or any one of them.[42]

For daughters there would be no grammar by Powell's guidelines. The consensus was that the professions were no place for women. Powell was addressing merchants, tradesmen, lawyers, and "private gentlemen"; he warned them not to imitate "greater personages," who might raise their daughters to

> glory their skill in music, the posture of their bodies, their knowledge in languages, the greatness and freedom of their spirits and their arts in arraigning of men's affections at their flattering faces. This is not the way to breed a private Gentleman's daughter.[43]

Comments on the raising of daughters appeared in almost every type of writing. A ballad, "The Virgin's A.B.C. or An Alphabet of Vertuous Admonitions for a Chaste, Modest, and Well-governed Maid," had a verse of advice for each letter of the alphabet. A few of the four-line stanzas began:

> All youthful virgins, to this song give ear . . .
> Bear not a scornful mind . . .
> Choose then a modest carriage . . .
> Disdainful never seem . . .
> Offend not with a foul and slandrous tongue . . .
> Paint not your beauty when it is decayed . . .
> Zealous then be in all these virtues, prove. . . .[44]

One early romantic tale, called *The Excellent Historye of Theseus and Ariadne,* included this severe and cynical "Rule for Women to Brynge up Their Daughters" in the introduction:

If they will go or gad abroad,
Their legs let broken be;
Put out their eyes if they will look
Or gaze undecently.[45]

Yet even advocates of the strictest upbringing for daughters admitted that it was unwise to keep them completely closeted and unfamiliar with social activities. This direction comes from *The Christen State of Matrimony,* a mid-sixteenth-century treatise on "How Daughters and Maidens Must Be Kept":

I [would] not have them ever shut up as it were in cage, never to speak nor to come forth, but some times to see the good fashions and honest behavior of other, for to keep them ever in mew [cooped up] is enough either to make them stark fools, or else to make them naughties when they shall once come abroad into company.[46]

With all this printed advice, was there in fact a solid consensus on how to raise, train, and educate daughters in that 150-year period from the reign of Henry VIII, through the Commonwealth, and well into the reign of Charles II? Hardly. Even within the separate classes that so divided the English people it is difficult to find consistent agreement. There were Puritans, Catholics, Quakers, and Anglicans in each class, and religion produced different ideas on how to raise daughters. There were country folk and city families, and their cultures differed. There were wealthy and prominent people who gathered at court, and there were other aristocratic families who stayed away from London (or Oxford, during the Civil War). There were those who favored serious intellectual schooling for girls and others who believed such training either was too much for female minds or would lead girls into lascivious thoughts or actions.

Some men complained that knowledge of the classics would encourage their wives to converse with priests and friars. Richard Hyrde, a supporter of classical studies for females, replied that a man could hardly find a better way to keep women from talking with churchmen because priests "abhorre and flye from" Latin and Greek and learning. This cynical and exaggerated remark was published in 1526, a few years before the break with the Roman Catholic church, a time when there was much criticism of both priests and the church hierarchy.[47]

Yet certain ideas found acceptance in nearly all of society. Patriarchy was one—a living, dominant cultural reality. The Bible taught that women were inferior to men and must obey the men under whose care they found themselves. The first thing a girl (or boy) learned was what was written in the Bible. Men held the leadership positions in their worlds. And boys were given privileges of education and inheritance not generally available to girls. A father or some other man held the right to control a female's life and property. Men possessed swords and bullets and were physically stronger. This sense of male dominance was unavoidable; all the classes taught that same message. A daughter—whether raised in a liberal-thinking family or the strictest religious setting—would learn about her so-called inferiority in the "Great Chain of Being." She might have power beyond the norm owing to her wealth or the family she was born into, but always the ultimate control was in the hands of the males. God was a "he"; no one proposed at that time that God was anything other than male.

Daughters also learned where they stood in the class society—to whom to doff their hats, as it were. This was an important concept in a society where servants could be whipped by their "betters" and wives could be legally beaten by their husbands, and even attendants at court had to know just where everyone stood in the hierarchy.

Religious training was another universal pattern. The basic tenets of Christianity (the only religion allowed) were supposed to be taught to every child. Everyone in a given geographical area was automatically a member of the local parish and required to attend church services. Absences were punishable by fines. Every village had its church and every church its preacher, who had a captive audience weekly for sermons or homilies that taught the church's creed. It was hard to avoid church dominance. And the church taught that women were secondary.

One skill seemed vital to every female. That was the use of needle and thread. The form needlework took would differ with the woman and her place in society, but writers agreed that women should know how to sew or create fine stitchery. It was essential work, and it kept idle hands busy. Few women were without their sewing or stitchery. It might consist of fine crewelwork for the noblewoman or basic clothes-making for the simplest family. But it was considered a good occupation for women, one that should be taught from an early age.

There was, then, much variation in the raising of daughters—except for the basic concepts of hierarchy, patriarchy, religion, and needlework. They could be vital to the upbringing of any daughter, and society taught them as much as did parents. Sewing and weaving were taught to poor and orphan girls in free schools where, to be sure, they would also learn about hierarchy, patriarchy, and the Bible.

Once departed for their new lives as married women, daughters might still receive directions from parents. This "Letter of Counsell from a Discreet Mother to her Daughter, Newly Married," appeared in a book of sample letters printed in 1615:

> My good daughter, thou art now going into the world and must leave to be a child, and learn to be a mother and to look to a family rather than to the entertainment of a friend . . . avoid tattling gossips yet be kind to thy neighbors and no stranger to thy kindred, be gentle to thy servants but not overfamiliar, have an eye to the door and a lock to thy chest, keep a bit for a beggar and a bone for a dog . . . take heed abroad of the kite and within of the rat.[48]

Those words, at least, might be good advice even today. ❦

Notes

1. *The Lisle Letters: An Abridgement*, ed. Muriel St. Clare Byrne (Chicago: Univ. Press, 1983), 201.
2. Thomas Becon, *The Catechism* (Cambridge: Univ. Press, 1844), 348.
3. *The Office of Christian Parents: Shewing How Children are to be Governed Throughout all Ages and Times of their Life* (1616), 60.
4. Alice Thornton, *The Autobiography of Alice Thornton* (The Surtees Society, 1875), 1.
5. Becon, 357.
6. Ibid., 366–72.
7. Ibid., 368.
8. Ibid., 371.
9. Ibid., 369.
10. *The Court of Good Counsell* (1607), H2^v.
11. Eustace Chapuys, Imperial Ambassador to Charles V, in *Great Britain Public Record Office*, Calendar of Letters and Papers, Foreign and Domestic, of the Reign of Henry VIII, reprint 1965, 8:101.
12. *The Court of Good Counsell*, H3.
13. Baldassare Castiglione, *The Courtyer* (reprinted as *The Book of the Courtier* in *The Tudor Translations*, Vol. 23, W. E. Henley, ed. (London: David Nutt, 1900), 215–16.
14. William Gouge, *Of Domesticall Duties* (1622), 534.
15. Retha M. Warnicke, "Lady Mildmay's Journal: A Study in Autobiography and Meditation in Reformation England" in *Sixteenth Century Journal*, Vol. 20,1 (1989): 58.
16. Thornton, 8.
17. Margaret M. Verney, *Memoirs of the Verney Family During the Commonwealth, 1650–1660: Compiled from the Letters and Illustrated by the Portraits at Claydon House* (London: Longmans, Green and Co., 1894), 3:72.
18. Ibid., 73–74.
19. Ibid., 74.
20. Thomas Salter, *A Mirrhor Mete for all Mothers, Matrones, and Maidens, Intituled the Mirrhor of Modestie* [1579], B2^v, B3. See Suzanne W. Hull, *Chaste, Silent & Obedient: English Books for Women 1475–1540* (San Marino, Calif.: Huntington Library Press, 1982, 1988), 58, for longer quotes from Salter.

21. Giovanni Michele Bruto, *The Necessarie, Fit, and Convenient Education of a Yong Gentlewoman* (1598), G2.
22. See Warnicke, 56–68.
23. Lisle, 87.
24. Ibid., 334.
25. Ibid., Chap. 10, "Careers for the Children," 191–211.
26. Martin Billingsley, *The Pens Excellencie* (1618), B4^v.
27. See Dorothy Gardiner, *English Girlhood at School: A Study of Women's Education through Twelve Centuries* (London: Oxford Univ. Press, 1929).
28. The [Roxburghe] Society, *Roxburghe Ballads* (1877), 3:38.
29. A., *The Passoinate [passionate] Morrice* (1593), H4^v.
30. David Cressy, "Literacy in Pre-Industrial England," in *Societas, A Review of Social History* 4 (Summer 1974): 229–40.
31. Desiderus Erasmus, *A Lytell Booke of Good Maners for Chyldren* (1532), C^v–C2^v.
32. Lisle, 198.
33. Becon, 372. See also "Rules for Wives" in this volume.
34. *Daughters, Wives, and Widows*, ed. Joan Larsen Klein (Urbana and Chicago: Univ. of Illinois Press, 1992), 6.
35. Thomas Carter, *Carters Christian Commonwealth or Domestical Dutyes Deciphered* (1627), 69.
36. Ibid., 123.
37. Roxburghe, 3, I:51–56.
38. Becon, 368.
39. Verney, 135.
40. Richard Allestree, *The Ladies Calling* (1673), 12.
41. Richard Mulcaster, *Positions . . . for the Training Up of Children* (1581), Abridged edition. ed. Richard L. DeMolen (New York: Teachers College Press, 1971), 83.
42. Thomas Powell, *Tom of All Trades* (1631), 46.
43. Ibid., 47.
44. Roxburghe, 651.
45. Thomas Underdowne, *The Excellent Historye of Theseus and Ariadne* (1566), [13].
46. Heinrich Bullinger, *The Christen State of Matrimony* [1541], M7^v.
47. Richard Hyrde, Introduction to Margaret More Roper's translation of Desiderius Erasmus, *A Devout Treatise upon the Pater Noster* (1526).
48. Cited in Katherine Gee Hornbeak, *The Complete Letter-Writer* (Northampton, Mass.: Smith College, 1934), 41.

Chapter Six

Preparing Food

Preparing Food

*T*he first printed cookbook in English appeared in 1500. It is known as a *Book of Cookery*, the name given to several of the early cookbooks. Typically for the time, it lacks a title page, but the first words, or incipit—which substitutes for a title—read:

> *Here begynneth a noble boke of festes ryalle and Cokery a boke for a pryncis housholde or any other estates . . .*[1]

This was hardly a practical guidebook for the average housewife. But it may have been of interest to those who wanted to know how the upper classes lived. Only a very grand household could use the enormous amounts of ingredients called for in some of the recipes; they were written for a chef preparing food for a castle or a good-sized manor house. Many of the ingredients, including rare spices, were expensive. A middle-class housewife, cooking for a few family members and servants, would hardly be concerned with making pies "that the birds [four-and-twenty?] may be alive in them and fly out when it is cut up."[2] Even less would they need this recipe for a huge "Oxfordshire Cake," found in the multieditioned *Compleat Cook*, published in 1655:

> Take a peck of flour by weight and dry it a little and a pound and a half of sugar, an ounce of cinnamon, half an ounce of nutmegs, a quarter of an ounce of mace and cloves, a good spoonful of salt. Beat your salt and spice very fine and searce [strain] it and mix it with your flour and

Opposite page:
WOMAN WITH ALEMBIC (DISTILLING APPARATUS), from *The Ladies Delight*, by Hannah Wolley (London, 1672). By permission of the British Library, 1037a37.

sugar. Then take three pounds of butter and work it in the flour. It will take three hours working, then take a quart of ale-yeast, two quarts of cream, half a pint of sack, six grains of ambergris [expensive, waxy secretion from sperm whales] dissolved in it, half a pint of rosewater, sixteen eggs, eight of the whites. . . . When you make it ready for your oven, put to your cake six pounds of currants, two pounds of raisins of the sun, stoned and minced. . . . It will take three hours baking.[3]

A number of early cookbooks were printed, ostensibly for use by the upper classes. But printers of cookbooks also played on middle-class readers' interest in royal and noble life. The recipes and menus gave insight into the food prepared and customs followed in affluent households. Some of the best-selling recipe books in the seventeenth century bore titles like *The Queens Closet Opened* and *The Queen-like Closet*, or they claimed to be the "secrets" of noblewomen like the Countess of Kent, whose books, published after her death, went into many editions. And many of the books were addressed to "Ladies and Gentlewomen." This snobbery—for "Ladies and Gentlewomen" referred strictly to members of the upper classes—appealed as well to middle-class readers. If you had the purchase money for *The Ladies Cabinet Enlarged and Opened*, or *A Delightfull Daily Exercise for Ladies and Gentlewomen*, or *Delightes for Ladies*, you did not have to *be* a lady or gentlewoman to buy and enjoy them.

Other recipe books were addressed specifically to housewives. Three of the earliest were *The Good Huswifes Jewell*, *The Good Hous-wives Treasurie*, and *The Treasurie of Commodious Conceits and Hidden Secrets and may be called, the Huswives Closet of Healthfull Provision*. These were tiny, pocket-sized volumes with scarcely two-by-four inches of type on each page. The type was sometimes further constricted by a decorative printed border.[4] These books were not just about food preparation. Medicinal cures (for livestock as well as people); formulas for preparing cosmetics; and directions for distilling waters, dyeing cloth, dieting, preventing drunkenness, and that recurrent direction "To Kill Lyce"—all were thrown in with food recipes.

The eating habits of the sixteenth and seventeenth centuries varied (as did so much of life) according to class. They also differed widely from those of today. The staple foods—for those who could afford it—were meat, fish, and fowl. Landowners could select from a great variety of domestic animals and wildlife. Cattle, sheep, and chickens were plentiful on their farms, while deer, rabbits, pheasants, salmon, and all kinds of other wild creatures were theirs for the netting or shooting on their own property. Not so for the poorer sort: they might own a cow or a few pigs and chickens, but much of the wildlife was considered to be the property of the landowner. Those who took it could be convicted of poaching, especially after antipoaching laws were strengthened around 1650.

Menus of feasts for the wealthy included endless lists of meats and milk products, though few vegetables. Root vegetables—especially onions, turnips, and parsnips—were used, as were a variety of herbs. But many popular green vegetables of today—such as brussels sprouts, green peppers, broccoli, and even green peas—were unknown or rarely mentioned. There are a number of recipes for artichokes. According to the television cook Delia Smith, artichokes used to be more popular in England than they are today.

Recipes for preserving cucumbers (spelled and pronounced "cowcumber" in the seventeenth century) amounted to pickle-making and differed little from today's method. Potatoes arrived on the European continent in the sixteenth century, but were not common in England until the mid-eighteenth century. However, the first female cookbook author, Hannah Wolley, included directions "To Make a Potato Pye" in her second book, *The Cooks Guide*, published in 1664:

> Scald them well and pill [peal] them; then put butter into your pye, then whole mace, then potatoes with marrow, cinnamon, mace and sugar, then butter. So close it and bake it, and when it is baked, put in some white wine, butter and sugar with the yolks of eggs.[5]

A decade later, William Rabisha described, in his *Whole Body of Cookery Dissected,* how "To Fry [Jerusalem?] Artichokes or Spanish Potatoes":

> When they are boiled and sliced fitting for that purpose, you must have your yolks of eggs beaten with a grated nutmeg or two. When your pan is hot you must dip them into the yolks of eggs and charge your pan. When they are fried on both sides your lear [sauce] to your artichokes is drawn butter and to your potatoes, butter, vinegar, sugar and rosewater. These for a need may serve for second course dishes.[6]

The Ladies Cabinet Enlarged and Opened explained how "To Make a Paste of Carrots," but the writer seemed uncertain just where and how to serve the dish:

> Take carrot roots, boil them, take out of the pith one pound, paring off all the outside, beat the pith in a mortar with half a pint of rose water. Then take one pound of sugar finely beaten, and the yolks of sixteen eggs, beat them with the carrots altogether, then put it in a dish and dry it, and being thus made into paste, put it to what use, or in what fashion you like best.[7]

Salad recipes appeared often, and commonly called for herbs and flowers, as in this recipe from the popular *English House-wife*:

> Of Compound [mixed] Salads: Your compound salads are first the young buds and knots of all manner of wholesome herbs at their first springing, as red sage, mints, lettuce, violets, marigolds, spinach, and many other mixed together and then served up to the table with vinegar, salad oil, and sugar.[8]

The same book—though addressed to housewives—had another, fancier salad recipe, "an excellent salad, and which indeed is usual at great feasts and upon princes' tables," again exploiting snob appeal. The recipe said to take

> a good quantity of blanched almonds, and with your shredding knife, cut them grossly. Then take as many raisins of the sun, clean washed, and the stones picked out, as many figs shredded like the almonds, as many capers, twice so many olives, and as many currants as of all the rest, clean washed, a good handful of the small tender leaves of red sage and spinach. Mix all these together with good store of sugar, and lay them in the bottom of a great dish.

This already sounds substantial. But there was more:

> Then put unto them vinegar and oil, and scrape more sugar over all. Then take oranges and lemons, and paring away the outward pills [skins], cut them into thin slices. Then with those slices cover the salad all over, which done take the fine thin leaf of the red cauliflower, and with them cover the oranges and lemons all over, then over those red leaves lay another course of old olives and the slices of well-pickled

cucumbers, together with the very inward heart of your cabbage lettuce, cut into slices. Then adorn the sides of the dish and the top of the salad with more slices of lemons and oranges, and so serve it up.[9]

This elegant dish was really a glorified fruit salad. Oddly, oranges in that time were more tart and less sweet than lemons. John Murrell, who published four cookbooks in the early seventeenth century, provides the explanation in this recipe:

To Make Paste of Lemons: Use them in all things as you did the oranges, but put not so much sugar by half for that the lemons are not so bitter as the oranges. Then box them and keep them for your use.[10]

The simpler, nonfruit salads might include the easy-to-grow radish. Many called for flowers, like this one from another of Murrell's books:

Salad of Rosebuds and Clove Gillyflowers [carnations]: Pick rosebuds and put them into an earthen pipkin [small cooking pot] with white wine, vinegar and sugar. So may you use cowslips [fragrant yellow flower that grows wild in pastures], violets or rosemary flowers.[11]

Flowers appear in many food concoctions. Roses, plentiful in the English countryside, were essential to the making of the ever-useful rosewater. Roses had to be plentiful to provide the *pound* of red rose leaves called for "To Make Conserve of Roses Boiled" in the eclectic *Queens Closet Opened:*

Take a quart of red rosewater, a quart of fair water, boil in the water a pound of red rose leaves, the whites cut off. The leaves must be boiled very tender. Then take three pounds of sugar, and put to it a pound at a time and let it boil a little between every pound, so put it up in your pots.[12]

One of Markham's recipes required a "thousand damask roses."[13] And *The Queens Closet Opened* also printed recipes for candying flowers:

Take the blossoms of diverse sorts of flowers and make a syrup of water and sugar and boil it very thick. Then put in your blossoms and stir them in their boiling till it turn to sugar again. Then stir them with the back of a spoon till the sugar fall from it. So may you keep them for salads all the year.[14]

Sugar, of course, was a vital ingredient in candying, but it was also prominent in other dishes: witness the salads mentioned above. England first became acquainted with sugar in the fourteenth century. It was expensive enough to be a luxury, costing up to one and a half shillings a pound in 1600. (The daily wage for an average laborer in the seventeenth century was no more than one shilling.)[15] By the late 1600s sugar was taxed; the tariff continued for nearly two centuries. But by 1700 the price of sugar had dropped substantially—a result of increased trade with the Near East—to six pence or less. Sugar was in any case common enough to appear frequently, and in large amounts, in recipe books of the sixteenth and seventeenth centuries. A writer who described himself as "that ever famous Thomas Muffett, Doctor in Physick" (and whose book, *Healths Improvement,* was said to be corrected and enlarged by another doctor who was a fellow of the "Colledg of Physitians in London"), produced an interesting work that describes and qualifies foods of all kinds as well as discussing diet and air. The book included a couple of pages on the various kinds of sugar in use in 1655:

> The best sugar is hard, solid, light, exceeding white and sweet, glistening like snow, close and not spongy, melting (as salt doth) very speedily in any liquor. Such cometh from Madera in little loaves of three or four pound weight apiece, from whence also we have a coarser sort of sugar loaves, weighing seven, eight, nine or ten pounds a piece, not fully so good for candying fruits, but better for syrups and kitchen uses.[16]

Muffett's book was not a recipe book, but the credentials of its author (as well as those of the book's "enlarger") put him in the rare position of being a qualified English physician writing for a lay audience on paramedical matters.

The poor—for whom meat as well as sugar was a luxury—scraped by largely on bread, lentils, oats, and (if they were lucky) a little cheese. Starvation, particularly in poor crop years, was often a reality. Their bread was made of the coarse grains—rye, oats, or barley. (The wealthy could choose wheat, which was made into white bread.) Some of the poor could eat meat on occasion, if they were lucky enough to own two or three animals. One animal could be slaughtered in the fall and salted (or "powdered," as salting was sometimes called) for use throughout the winter. Salting was the most common method of preserving meat. (Canning and freezing were yet unheard of, so householders had limited means of preservation.) But one recipe explained "How to Keep Meat Fresh and Sweet a Long Time Without Salt":

> Put your meat in flour, meal or bran and therein it will keep fresh and sweet a long time, or else cast beaten coriander seed and vinegar on it, and it will do the same.[17]

Another way was to put the cooked meat in a pot and stop it up with melted butter, which would form an airtight seal.

The books abound with directions for cooking meat, fowl, and fish. Recipes range from simple boiling to intricate techniques from foreign lands. Here is a fairly sophisticated method of preparing "Boiled Meats for Dinner," taken from *The Good Huswifes Jewell*, a late-sixteenth-century recipe book:

> Take the ribs of a neck of mutton and stuff it with marjoram, savory, thyme, parsley chopped small, currants, with the yolks of two eggs, pepper and salt. Then put it into a posnet [small pot] with fair water, or else with the liquor of some meat, with vinegar, pepper and salt, and a little butter, and so serve it.[18]

Epulario, an Italian cookbook translated into English in 1598, provided many of the more exotic recipes. It also gave readers an idea of the wide variety of fowl that could be presented for a meal:

> Shoveler [waterfowl], puet [peewee], duck, crane, wild goose, heron and stork, are all good and would be stuffed with garlick, onions, or such like things. Peacock, pheasant, partridge, wild hen, quaile, thrush, blackbird, and all other good birds are to be roasted. Pigeons are good both roasted and sodden [boiled], yet best roasted. King doves and wild pigeons are good roasted, but better boiled with pepper, sage, parsley, and marjoram. Capon is good both boiled and roasted, and likewise the hen.[19]

The term "pie" was primarily reserved for those made of meat or fowl; dessert pies (usually without top crusts) were called, as they still are, "tarts." Judging by the recipe books, meat pies were popular. *The*

Ladies Cabinet Enlarged and Opened has this recipe telling "How to Bake a Steak Pie":

> Cut a neck of mutton in steaks, beat them with a cleaver, season them with pepper and salt and nutmeg, then lay them in your coffin [pie crust] with butter and large mace, then bake it. Then take a good quantity of parsley and boil it, beat it as soft as the pulp of an apple, put in a quarter of a pint of vinegar, and as much white wine (with a little sugar), warm it well, and pour it over your steaks, then shake it, that the gravy and liquor may mingle together. Scrape on sugar and serve it.[20]

Again, sugar is a prominent ingredient, as it is in this tempting dessert, "A Tart of Strawberries," from the same 1654 book.

> Pick and wash your strawberries very clean, and put them in your paste one by another as thick as you can. Then take sugar, cinnamon and a little ginger, finely beaten, and well mingled together, cast them upon the strawberries and cover them with the lid [top crust] finely cut into lozenges [latticework design] and so let it bake a quarter of an hour. Then take it out, and strewing it with a little cinnamon and sugar, serve it.[21]

Most fruit had to be used when it ripened, though some was dried for later use. For example:

> How to Keep Apples, Pears, Quinces, Wardens [baking pears], etc. All the Year Dry: Pare them, take out the cores, and slice them in thin slices, laying them to dry in the sun in some stone or metalline dishes, or upon an high frame covered with coarse canvas, now and then turning them, and so they will keep all the year.[22]

A Closet for Ladies and Gentlewomen had a strange suggestion about preserving cherries:

> Take of your fairest cherries you can get, but be sure that they be not bruised, and take them & rub them with a linen cloth, and put them into a barrel of hay, and lay them in ranks, first laying hay in the bottom, and then cherries, & then hay again, and then stop them up close that no air may come near them, and lay them under a featherbed where one lyeth continually, for the warmer they are, the better, yet near no fire, and thus doing you may have cherries at any time of the year.[23]

Although the English sweet tooth was not yet highly developed, books of the time offered various recipes for custards, cakes, tarts, puddings, "marchpane" (marzipan), fruit conserves, trifles, and candied flowers, plus directions for a rice pudding similar to today's:

> Take thin cream or good milk of what quantity you please, boil it on the fire with a little cinnamon in it, and when it hath boiled a while, take out the cinnamon and put in rosewater and sugar enough to make it good and sweet. Then having your rice ready beaten as fine as flour (and searced [strained] as some do it) strow it in till it be of the thickness of a hasty pudding. Then pour it into a dish and serve it to the table.[24]

Usually a hasty pudding meant flour boiled in water or milk; in New England it took the form of cornmeal mush. Directions for a rather elaborate hasty pudding "that will butter itself" can be found in Hannah Wolley's *Cooks Guide:*

> Take a quart of cream and boil it with grated bread, and as many plumped currants as you shall think fit, with some spice and a little salt; when you perceive it to be enough, put in the yolks of four eggs well beaten, and a little rosewater and sugar; then let it boil a very little, and turn it out into a dish, and serve it in.[25]

Several of the earliest printed cookbooks recited "the order of meats, how they must be served at the table." These menus, directed at the nobility, could be of astonishing length and variety. This one is from the 1629 *Booke of Cookerie and the Order of Meates to bee Served to the Table*:

> Services for Flesh Dayes at Dinner. The First Course: Pottage of stewed broth, boiled meat or stewed meats, chickens and bacon, powdered [salted] beef, pies, goose, pig, roasted beef, roasted veal, custard. The Second Course: Roasted lamb, roasted capons, roasted conger [large saltwater eel], chickens, peahens, baked venison, tart.

> The First Course at Supper: A salad, pigs pettitoes [pig's feet, sometimes internal organs as well], powdered beef sliced, a shoulder of mutton or a breast [of] veal, lamb, custard. The Second Course: Capons roasted, congers roasted, chickens roasted, pigeons roasted, larks roasted, a pie of pigeons or chickens, baked venison, tart.

The Service at Dinner: A dozen quails, a dish of larks, two pasties of red deer in a dish, tart, ginger-bread, fritters.[26]

The menus would list what was appropriate on fish days as well. These serving lists provide clues to eating customs and show the formality that was part of life in noble and wealthy households.

Fowl—from songbirds to swans—were part of the upper-class diet. A curious description was repeated in several early cookbooks:

Lift that swan, unlace that cony, display that crane, disfigure that peacock, untag that curlew, alay that pheasant, wing that partridge, mince that plover.[27]

"Lift," "unlace," "display," "disfigure," and so on, all meant "carve."

But what of the less glamorous meals prepared daily by commoners? Recipe books addressed to housewives give an idea of the foods that ordinary people might have cooked or preserved—everything from candied flowers and "marchpane" to common meats and salads—yet there are curious gaps. These books often lack recipes for common dishes, on the assumption that every woman would know how to prepare certain simple things. (In much the same way, descriptions on how to distill water or swaddle a baby were omitted from instruction books, on the ground that everyone already knew how to do such things. See the "Care of Babies" and "Health Habits and Household Remedies" chapters in this book.) The men who wrote or compiled these cookbooks may have assumed that any woman would know the basics. For instance, bread even then was "the staff of life," yet few if any recipes tell how to make the "black" bread eaten by most people. It was baked with the coarser grains: barley, rye, maslin (a mixture of grains—or "corn," the British term), even bean flour. The easy explanation is that people forced to eat the coarser breads probably did not spend much time with books, while middle-class housewives would shun such lowly fare.

Occasional recipes do appear for finer breads—including "manchet," a bread made of choice wheat flour. These directions may have worked with both coarse and fine flour. One recipe called for half a peck of flour (a peck is eight quarts), to which were added eight eggs; another had half a pound of sugar and four eggs, with the dough baked in a mold. These breads sound more like cake; apparently the eggs provided the leavening.

Beer, ale, and mead were often brewed at home for family consumption (and sometimes for sale), yet few recipes in the books show how the drinks were concocted. The know-how was instead passed down through generations. Mead, a common breakfast drink, had to be brewed frequently. One recipe said to boil honey and water with nutmeg and ginger and let it stand a week or two, but cautioned that it "will not keep long."[28] Metheglin, a stronger variety of mead, was a Welsh drink that added herbs to the mixture. Most of the mildly alcoholic drinks were vital parts of the daily menu. All provided calories in relatively unpolluted liquids.

Then there are recipes for a number of dishes rarely known today, except as they can be resurrected through *The Oxford English Dictionary*. Examples are: "To Boil a Breame" (a fresh-water fish), "To Make an Apple Moyse" (a kind of fried custard), "To Make White Estings" (probably Isings—puddings stuffed like sausages), and "To Make Andolians" (Andouilles, a dish consisting of hogs' guts, bacon, spices, and herbs). There were also ways to cook wardens (baking pears), medlars (fruits resembling small brown apples), and hyppes (rose hips). Some of the cooking terms are obsolete. Seething (boiling) was a common form of preparation that left food sodden. A leach was either a slice of food, usually meat, or a dish of cold cuts. A coffin was a piecrust. Verjuice or, as it was usually spelled, vergice was a liquor made of sour fruit. This recipe used verjuice in the boiling process:

> To Boyle a Pigs Petitoes [pig's foot]: Take and boil them in a pint of vergice and bastard [sweet Spanish wine]. Take four dates minced with a few small raisins. Then take a little thyme and chop it small and season it with a little cinnamon and ginger and a quantity of vergice.[29]

Boiling must have been the easiest method of preparing meat, judging by the number of recipes for "seething" or "sodden" food. A wide variety of ingredients could be added to the water. A boiled capon, for example, might have been prepared with syrup, oranges, lemons, almonds, herbs, eggs, currants, and butter, or in a pot with salt beef and wine.[30]

As far as is known, no woman took credit for any recipe books in her own lifetime until Hannah Wolley published her *Ladies Directory* in

1661, soon followed by her *Cooks Guide*. Men wrote or assembled the vast bulk of them. Even those books whose titles implied royal or aristocratic feminine connections were produced by men. *The Queens Closet Opened* purported to include elegant recipes from Queen Henrietta Maria's private collections, but its author is the anonymous W. M. (Of course, it is conceivable that W. M. was a woman.) The first of its many editions did not appear until 1655 when the dowager queen was in exile in her native France. The many editions of two other popular recipe books, purported to be by Elizabeth Grey, the Countess of Kent, were all published after the death of the countess. One male author allowed that he merely reorganized the manuscript of a highly respected woman, though the woman's name does not appear. Presumably her name did not carry the cachet of a royal or noble title, so he published under his own name. Another man admitted in a preface that he had never made any of his cheese recipes, but had "seen much made." *The Treasurie of Commodious Conceits* has a frontispiece of a man—perhaps the author, John Partridge—shown writing at a desk. In giving their names to cookbooks, men positioned themselves as instructors to women whether the recipes were theirs or not. They chose the recipes and thus determined the printed instructions that literate housewives might use.

The precise measurements and careful directions of modern cookbooks were unknown in most Tudor-Stuart publications. Instead, recipes frequently used general instructions, such as "take of your fairest cherries" or "Take almonds . . . and strain them together with milk and water," leaving the exact amounts to the imagination or experience of the cook. The recipe for the "Oxfordshire Cake," quoted at the beginning of this chapter, is exceptionally exact, with its peck of flour, three pounds of butter, and six pounds of currants. The lack of specific measurements in most recipes may have to do with the biases of the writers. Men writing the recipe books may have seen their task as one of compiling general information for their readers, relying on women cooks to supply the details. Or, when not cooks themselves, as was often the case, they may simply have underestimated the importance of measurements.

Recipes were always written in a narrative form that could fill up to three pages, somewhat like a story. In fact, the cookbooks may have seemed a fantasy to many who owned them, with their descriptions of food and life in inaccessibly aristocratic and wealthy homes. *A Book of Fruits and Flowers Shewing the Nature and Use of Them, either for Meat or Medicine* even had illustrations—simple drawings of the fruits and flowers described.

It is hard to draw accurate conclusions by studying the recipes alone. Often, the cookbooks were compilations of handwritten recipes from women as well as male chefs. Some men may have copied down recipes recited to them by women who had learned them orally. The recipes might neglect to cover the basic dishes of a middle-class home, particularly if they were written for snob appeal. The most common kitchen foods may also have been overlooked as too much a part of every household to need mentioning. For example, cheese was a staple, yet (with the exception of the man who had "seen much made") there were few directions for making it.

Yet some pictures emerge from these recipe books. It is clear that meat, fish, and birds comprised an important part of the diets of those who could acquire them. It is also clear that green vegetables played a minor role. Herbs, however, were plentiful. So were some spices, though their expense limited their use in poorer households. There were fruits in season, and occasionally dried fruit off-season. Distilling was an important activity in the home, not only to create the daily alcoholic drinks, but to prepare purified water as well. Sugar slowly became a mainstay. Almonds appeared in an astonishing number of recipes.[31]

The people of the burgeoning towns and cities were becoming specialized in their pursuits, and this applied to food preparation as well. In London, Samuel Pepys, the diarist, notes that his wife took the "joint" *out* to be cooked. In villages, households were largely self-sufficient, growing and preparing their own food. Still, a good baker or ale-maker could thrive there as well as in the city.

Although cookbooks were published exclusively by men until the latter part of the seventeenth century, women did pen private manuscripts of recipes. Some of them undoubtedly were the sources for cookbooks published under men's names. Other private manuscripts survive and continue to surface for study and comparison of the cooking and eating habits of people of the period. ❦

Notes

1. E. Gordon Duff, *Fifteenth Century English Books* (London: Oxford Univ. Press, 1917), 14.
2. *Epulario, or, the Italian Banquet* (1598), Biiii.
3. W. M., *The Compleat Cook* (1659), 13.
4. A good example is *A Closet for Ladies and Gentlewomen* (1608 and later editions).
5. Hannah Wolley, *The Cooks Guide* (1664), 86.
6. William Rabisha, *The Whole Body of Cookery Dissected* (1675), 107.
7. M. B., *The Ladies Cabinet Enlarged and Opened* (1654), 24.
8. Gervase Markham, *The English House-wife* (1631), 66.
9. Ibid.
10. John Murrell, *A Delightful Daily Exercise for Ladies and Gentlewomen* (1621), D11.
11. John Murrell, *Murrells Two Books of Cookerie and Carving* (1638), 38.
12. W. M., *The Queens Closet Opened* (1655), 209.
13. Markham, 118.
14. W. M., 240.
15. Mildred Campbell, *The English Yeoman Under Elizabeth and the Early Stuarts* (New York: Augustus M. Kelley, 1968), 215.
16. Thomas Muffett, *Healths Improvement: or, Rules Comprizing and Discovering the Nature, Method, and Manner of Preparing all Sorts of Food Used in this Nation* (1655), 250.
17. Francis Dickinson, *A Pretious Treasury of Twenty Rare Secrets* (1649), A3^v.
18. Thomas Dawson, *The Good Huswifes Jewell* (1596), 6.
19. *Epulario, B*^{v}.
20. M. B., 211.
21. Ibid., 213.
22. Ibid., 20.
23. *A Closet for Ladies and Gentlewomen*, 65.
24. *The Ladies Cabinet Opened* (1637), 39.
25. Hannah Wolley, *The Cooks Guide* (1664), 80. The original punctuation is copied in this recipe to give a sense of the different way of structuring sentences.

26. *A Booke of Cookerie and the Order of Meates to bee Served to the Table, Both for Flesh and Fish Dayes* (1629), A2. This is a later interpretation of several sixteenth-century cookbooks. See also (if you can find them) Dawson's cookbooks and several so-called books of cookery.
27. From *Here Begynneth the Boke of Kervynge* (1508) as quoted in Arnold Whitaker Oxford, *English Cookery Books to 1850* (London, etc.: Oxford Univ. Press, 1913), 2.
28. Robert May, *The Accomplisht Cook* (1660), 261.
29. *A Book of Cookerie*, 9.
30. Ibid., 12–13.
31. Helpful details on food use in the Tudor-Stuart period can be found in J. C. Drummond and A. Wilbraham, *The Englishman's Food: A History of Five Centuries of English Diet* (London: Jonathan Cope, 1958); Dorothy Hartley, *Food in England* (London: Macdonald, 1979); and Peter Brears et al, *A Taste of History: 10,000 Years of Food in Britain* (London: English Heritage/British Museum Press, 1993).

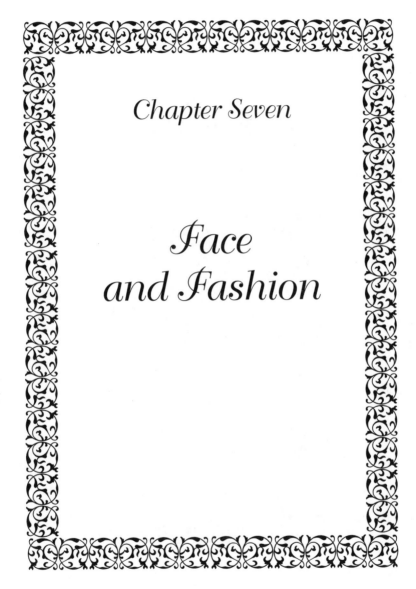

Chapter Seven

Face
and Fashion

Face and Fashion

*P*ortraits of the wives and daughters of Henry VIII show a growing extravagance in female fashions at the sixteenth-century English court. Later royal portraits demonstrate the same for the seventeenth century. Yet none of these paintings hints at the widespread criticism (in print and pulpit) of elaborate, ostentatious and expensive dress. Though critics did not aim many barbs at the royal family, they did rail at extravagant clothes, unnatural curves, painted faces, and false or dyed hair, especially on women of the middle class. Repeated efforts were made to control female appearance.

Class was the key. Court and clergy both tried, by statute and sermon, to persuade men and women to dress only in a manner suitable to their positions in life. What was acceptable for courtiers was not acceptable for the middle class. William Gouge, in his lengthy matrimonial guide first published in 1622, explained:

> One end of apparel is to show a difference betwixt superiors and inferiors, persons in authority and under subjection.[1]

Proper clothing for each rank made it easier to see at a glance who was who in the hierarchy. A style that mimicked the court was declared unseemly or sinful in a proper Puritan family. It might also be judged illegal.

Opposite page:
ORNATELY DRESSED WOMAN, from *A Discourse Against Painting and Tincturing of Women* by Thomas Tuke (London, 1616). By permission of The Huntington Library, San Marino, Calif.

A number of "Statutes of Apparel" were issued in the sixteenth century. These royal edicts spelled out in detail the dress codes for men and women of various ranks and classes. For example, certain rich fabrics and furs could be used only by the nobility, and there were distinctions even among the highest class. A 1574 statute read:

> None shall wear any cloth of gold, tissue, nor fur of sables except duchesses, marquises and countesses in their gowns, kirtles [skirts], partlets [neckerchiefs] and sleeves.[2]

Velvet, leopard fur, or silk embroidery could be used in gowns worn by ladies of highest ranks as well as wives of barons' sons or knights, but by no others. Another statute forbade anyone below the rank of "wife of a gentleman bearing arms" to wear damask, tufted taffeta, or grosgrain. This decree made an exception for wives whose families "may dispend 40 pounds by the year," and other statutes allowed the wealthy, regardless of rank, to wear certain fabrics. Class distinctions were blurring; wealth was growing in importance.

Many of the laws were modified as fashions changed. In 1580 one law banned the use of "excessive long cloaks . . . or . . . such great and excessive ruffs . . . as had not been used before two years past." Punishment could be severe: fines and imprisonment as well as forfeiture of the offending clothes apparel. But judging by the number of repeated proclamations on clothing, largely during Queen Elizabeth's reign, many people ignored the laws.

This was a time when wealthy men and courtiers were as dressy as women. In the Elizabethan period they exposed their legs to the upper thighs in tight-fitting stockings beneath bulbous bloomers. They sported rich fabrics and furs, bright colors, and—in the next century—favored oversized hats, wigs, and colored hair. Even the clergy wore gorgeous clothes. Not so for the "common sort" of people. For them the length of coats, and even suitable colors, were regulated, the better to tell at a glance where the person stood in the hierarchy. Apprentices wore blue; servants wore only short gowns.

Flamboyantly dressed men received some share of criticism, but women were the more likely targets in sermons and marriage guides. Controlling their garments was one way of controlling what some people felt to be a growing decadence among women. They were criticized for spending too much money on clothes while covering less of their bodies. A few years after Elizabeth became queen, Thomas Becon wrote:

> It shall not be unfitting that all honest and godly-disposed maids content themselves with comely and seemly apparel, even such as becometh their degree, state, vocation and calling, utterly rejecting and casting away all nice vanity and vain niceness of apparel, according to the doctrine of the gospel.[3]

The Bible was the source of Becon's (and many others') thinking. Becon quoted Saint Paul (1 Timothy 2:9):

> I will . . . that the women array themselves in comely apparel, with shamefacedness [shyness] and discrete behaviour, not with braided hair, gold, or pearls or costly array.[4]

Becon went so far as to say that Saint Paul "meaneth also maids and all of the womankind." The queen and most of her courtiers ignored him.

There was widespread fear that women might entrap men with voluptuous clothing, false hair, and painted faces. Some were accused of spending too much time and money on appearance and ignoring the word of God. Writers preached that true beauty was in goodness and godliness, not in external impressions: "The beauty of behavior is more precious in estimation than the beauty of the body."[5] All women did not agree. Despite the frequent warnings, many women (if they could afford them) wore fine dresses and jewels. Bewailing bygone days, Barnabe Rich, a prolific early professional writer, wrote in 1616:

> It was a happy age when a man might have wooed his wench with a pair of kid-leather gloves, a silver thimble or with a tawdry lace. But now a velvet gown, a chain of pearl or a coach with four horses will scarcely serve the turn.

And:

> It was a merry world when seven or eight yards of velvet would have made a gown for a Lady of honor. Now eighteen will not suffice for her that is scarce worthy to be a good Lady's laundress.[6]

Although it often took more material to make a fashionable dress, it might nonetheless fail to cover as much of the body as some thought seemly. Extreme decolletage and bared breasts were seen. Queen Elizabeth, late in life, is reported to have opened her clothing to her waist during a formal interview with the French ambassador:

> She kept the front of her dress open, and one could see the whole of her bosom, and passing low, and often she would open the front of this robe with her hands as if she was too hot. . . . Her bosom is somewhat wrinkled . . . but lower down her flesh is exceeding white and delicate, so far as one could see.[7]

One seventeenth-century writer, John Bulwer, wrote a long book condemning fashions and cultural practices that distorted the human body. The book, with the tongue-twisting title of "*Anthropometamorphosis: Man Transformed,*" criticized the wheel farthingale, for example, because it greatly exaggerated a woman's hips. (Women trying to wear these elaborate fashions might well have agreed, since they made movement and sitting a challenge.) Bulwer's argument, echoed by other critics, was that God created the body as He thought best. The purpose of clothing, then, was to cover nakedness, not to alter or glorify the body.

Another glamorizing—or disfiguring—tool used by fashion-conscious women was the corset. Some were designed to create an elongated figure and a flattened bust, in imitation of the naturally thin Queen Elizabeth; others pinched the waist. The more costly corsets were made of metal, the cheaper ones of wood. No wonder it was easier, when corseted, to sit on a stool than in an armchair and simpler to stand than to sit. Concerning uncomfortable and unnatural clothing, John Bulwer said, scornfully:

> This ridiculous folly of affecting new shapes, or rather disguises of apparel, hath been taken notice of and condemned by many.[8]

But fancy clothing was only part of the problem, warned critics. Some preached loud and long against the use of cosmetics: these, they claimed, also distorted the natural look. Thomas Tuke's book *A Discourse Against Painting and Tincturing of Women*, published in 1616, scoffed at beauty aids that changed the color of the skin. (It should be noted that the translator was a woman, Elizabeth Arnold.) The book described facial cosmetics as:

> Paintings laid one upon another, in such sort that a man might easily cut off a curd or cheese cake from either of their cheeks.[9]

Nonetheless, how-to guides published more and more recipes for cosmetics and perfumes. Queen Elizabeth was a heavy user of cosmetics, and others followed suit. The queen suffered a severe case of smallpox when she was twenty-nine, which left her face scarred. She coated it with thick cosmetics to cover blemishes and create a fashionable, smooth, white skin. Others followed her lead. There were several ideas on how to reproduce this pale complexion. One recipe that might have generated those thick "cheese cakes" or "curds" of facial paste appeared in the popular *Closet for Ladies and Gentlewomen,* the versatile book that went into many editions (though all appeared after Queen Elizabeth's death):

> Take fresh bacon grease and the whites of eggs and stamp them together and a little powder of bays and annoint your face therewith, and it will make it white.[10]

A man named Hugh Platt produced another popular, pocket-sized recipe book around 1600. In it he, too, offered a plan for whitening the face. This one—"A White Fucus [paint] or Beauty for the Face"—may be less thick, but hardly more appealing:

> The jaw bones of a hog or sow well burned, beaten and searced [sifted] through a fine sieve and after ground upon a porphiry [slab for grinding drugs] . . . is an excellent fucus, being laid on with the oil of white poppy.[11]

Cosmetics inspired rhymes and jests as well as sermons. Tuke felt this way about fucus:

> Fucus is paint, and fucus is deceit,
> And fucus they use, that do mean to cheat.
> Methinks the very name should stir up shame,
> And make it hateful to each modest dame.[12]

John Taylor, the "Water Poet" and a famed humorist of his time, also panned face painting:

A skillful painter was requested to paint out a fair courtesan (in plain English, a whore). I pray you spare that cost, said the painter, for if she be a right whore she daily paints herself.[13]

One of the complaints about cosmetics was that they hid natural blushing, and blushing was a sign of a modest and properly "shame-fast" female. Tuke's *Discourse Against Painting and Tincturing of Women* explains:

It is not enough to be good, but she that is good must seem good; she that is chaste must seem chaste; she that is humble must seem humble; she that is modest must seem to be so and not plaster her face [so] that she cannot blush.[14]

This stricture was important in all phases of female life: not only must the woman act in accord with male (and generally accepted) cultural prescriptions, she must *appear* to be doing so as well. In other words, the proper woman should never flirt, or use cosmetics, or talk in a manner that would cause others around her to question her virtue. As Barnabe Rich put it:

The blush of a woman's face is an approbation of a chaste and an honest mind. . . . The woman that forgetteth to blush, it is an argument that she is past grace.[15]

Because of certain fashions, men also ran the danger of being deceived as to the true appearance of a woman. Richard Brathwaite, author of several books with moral undertones, warned that a close examination of certain so-called beauties would reveal that:

The hair she wears came from the periwig-makers shop. . . . Her eyes have no other brows than those which a pencil makes, nor her face no other color than that of painting. . . . If she would suffer her face to be washed, thou wouldst know her no more. She would be hideous unto thee. . . . If thou shouldst kiss her, all thy lips would be stuck with oil and grease; embrace her, and she is nought but pasteboard, canvas & whalebone with which all the body of her gown (the better body of the two) is stuffed to repair the faults of her proportion; and when she goes to bed, she leaves upon the table . . . half of her person in putting off her clothes.[16]

Regardless, some women continued to ape the court with beauty aids. If they did not actually paint their faces white, they were still anxious to have a fair complexion, free of freckles and pimples. One of the simplest recipes for clear skin was to "take fresh bean blossoms and distill them in a limbeck [distilling device] and with the water wash your face."[17] Another called for almonds blended with egg yolks as a paste "To Make One's Hands and Face Smooth and Fair." It also suggested that "To wear dog leather gloves is likewise good for that purpose,"[18] an interesting insight on the use—or misuse—of dogs. "A Fair Face" might also be achieved by washing it with a mixture of white vinegar and plantain herb, and then drinking "a draught of vinegar" every three days.[19]

Freckles were considered a blemish, and there were several remedies in seventeenth-century books. One used "May dew,"[20] another suggested the sap of a birch tree tapped in March or April,[21] and a third called for water of elder leaves distilled in May.[22] All three claimed to clear the skin of freckles. Unanswered was what to do if freckles appeared at any time other than spring.

There were also cures for pimples, such as:

Take bayberries and pluck off the husks, & make fine powder thereof, & temper it with honey & anoint thy face therewith six times, and it will help you.[23]

Perhaps the best recipe was the simplest:

To help a face that is red or pimpled, dissolve common salt in the juice of lemons, and with a linen cloth, pat the patient's face that is full of heat or pimples. It cureth in a few dressings.[24]

Hair length was a divisive topic then as now. In his book *Anthropometamorphosis*, author John Bulwer claimed that, "For men to nourish long hair is quite contrary to the intention of nature." He claimed that some people used hair "to wipe their hands from the fat and dirt of their meals." But he concluded that hair styles would differ with climate and custom, and decided, "Hair, long or short, thick or thin, more or less, is a matter of indifference."[25] Tastes varied widely. Some people favored more hair; others wanted less, particularly in certain places. Some wanted a different color; others preferred wigs. Some felt that women's hair should be long and men's short; others favored curled and coifed hair for men. In other words, it was the same debate that goes on today, except that long hair for men was touted by conservatives. The length and cut of men's hair denoted class as well as political and religious persuasion. This was particularly true in the mid-seventeenth century, when the Round Heads—Cromwell's sympathizers with bowl-cut hair—came to blows with the Royalists, who fancied longer styles. Tradesmen usually wore short hair. After the Restoration in 1660, wigs became more popular among the leisure class. This fashion usually required shaved heads.

Another fashion problem was baldness, which generated much advice. In 1649 *A Pretious Treasury of Twenty Rare Secrets* had a remedy:

> Take bees and burn them upon a fire shovel or such a thing. Then boil the ashes of the bees in salad oil. Then anoint therewith the place where you would have hair to grow and you shall obtain your wish within a short time.[26]

A 1661 recipe in the multi-faceted *Queens Closet Opened,* "To make hair grow thick," sounds sticky, scratchy, and improbable:

> Take three spoonfuls of honey and a good handful of vine sprigs that twist like wire, and beat them well and strain their juice into the honey, and anoint the bald places therewith.[27]

(Perhaps a few twisted sprigs might have stood up in the honey base and given an impression of hair for an hour or two.)

Women, on the other hand, were more concerned with getting rid of unwanted hair. One way to achieve it was to do as fashion-conscious foreigners did and pluck or remove hair from the forehead hairline. According to Bulwer, "The English commonly love a high forehead."[28] But not all fathers approved. One said:

> Fair daughters, see that you pluck not away the hairs from your eyebrows, nor from your temples, nor from your foreheads, to make them appear higher than nature ordained.[29]

Despite the warning, daughters (and other females) could find numerous recipes to eliminate offending hairs. One, printed about 1586, said to shave the spot and apply the blood of a black otter.[30] In the next century *The Queens Closet Opened* suggested two approaches:

> Take the shells of fifty-two eggs, beat them small, and still [distill] them with a good fire, and with the water anoint yourself where you would have the hair off. Or else cat's dung that is hard and dried, beaten to powder, and tempered with strong vinegar, and anointed on the place.[31]

Hair color could be important; in women it was sometimes considered an indication of character. Families seeking wet nurses for their babies were cautioned to avoid red-haired nurses.[32] Black-haired women, who were thought to be lustful, could try a recipe "To color a black hair presently into a chestnut color," which appeared in Platt's *Delightes for Ladies*. The recipe used oil of vitriol [sulphuric acid], "but you must do it very carefully, not touching the skin."[33] Platt said you could "Color the head or beard into a chestnut color in half an hour" by taking

> one part of lead calcined with sulphur, and one part of quicklime, temper them somewhat thin with water, lay it upon the hair, chasing it well in, and let it dry one quarter of an hour or thereabout. Then wash the same off with fair water divers times, and lastly with soap and water, and it will be a very natural hair color. The longer it lyeth upon the hair the browner it groweth. This coloreth not the flesh at all, and yet it lasteth very long in the hair.[34]

If, on the other hand, black were desired (usually for a man), a reader could use this suggestion from *A Pretious Treasury of Twenty Rare Secrets*:

> Take a little aqua fortis, put therein a groat or sixpence, according to the quantity of the foresaid water. Then set both to dissolve before the fire. Lastly, dip a little sponge in the said water, and wet your beard or hair therewith, but touch not the skin.[35]

Men and women of means followed the latest fashions and hoped to be among the first to wear the newest styles in hair and dress. This was an expensive undertaking. One of the reasons for the apparel statutes, said the queen herself, was to keep courtiers from overspending on fashion. Still the fads continued. Fashion-conscious women tried to mimick the queen's thin, flat torso by forcing their bodies into corsets of iron or wood panels, laced at the back. They also aped the queen's farthingales, wearing excessively wide hoops that made sitting a difficult feat. Others reshaped their bodies with cage-like corsets that attempted to minimize the waist.

Between roughly 1570 and 1620 one trend that received much attention in print was crossdressing by both men and women. This, claimed the moralists, threatened a necessary distinction between the sexes. Juan Luis Vives proclaimed, "A woman shall not put on man's apparel, for so to do is abominable before God."[36] At least one man cross-dressed to gain admission to an all-female gathering (a birthing).[37] Though it was not a widespread practice, enough women wore men's clothing in the early part of the seventeenth century to inspire at least one play (Thomas Middleton and Thomas Dekker's *The Roaring Girl*), two books (*Hic Mulier: Or, The Man-Woman* and *Haec-Vir: Or, The Womanish Man,* both published in 1620), and some curious drawings of clothing worn upside down and of male haircuts on females. Male clothing was worn occasionally by women as a disguise (as with some of Shakespeare's female characters), perhaps to gain employment in a male field of work, or even to go soldiering. Cross-dressing by women may also have been an expression of independence, or a means to shock, or just for fun. Instead of wooden corsets and layer upon layer of skirts and broad starched ruffs, the often simpler male clothes offered more comfort and ease of movement.

On the other hand, little boys traditionally wore skirts until age six or seven, when they were "breeched."

Trends in clothing and cosmetics were fickle then as now. Opinions on the most desirable shape for the female body kept changing as well. Finally, whatever the fashion, women (and men) worried about their weight. They lacked the diet pills and books of today, but they did have at least one recipe "For to Make One Slender":

> Take fennel and seeth it in water, a very good quantity, and wring out the juice thereof when it is sod [boiled], and drink it first and last, and it shall swage [quench the appetite of] either him or her.[38]

Who knows? Perhaps it works as well as some modern ideas. ❦

Notes

1. William Gouge, *Of Domesticall Duties* (1622), 602.
2. P. F. Hughes and J. F. Larkin, *Tudor Royal Proclamations* (1969), 385.
3. Thomas Becon, *The Catechism* (Cambridge: Univ. Press, 1844), 370; originally in his Workes (1560–1564), cccccxxxvi^v [cccccxxxii^v].
4. Ibid.
5. Barnabe Rich, *The Honestie of this Age* (1614), 34.
6. Rich, *My Ladies Looking Glasse* (1616), 19
7. The description of the queen was recorded in the journal of the Ambassador of the French King Henry IV and repeated in Louis Adrian Montrose, "'Shaping Fantasies': Figurations of Gender and Power in Elizabethan Culture" in *Representations* (Spring 1983, No. 2), 63.
8. John Bulwer, *Anthropometamorphosis: Man Transformed* (1653), 551.
9. Thomas Tuke, *A Discourse Against Painting and Tincturing of Women* (1616), B3^v.
10. *A Closet for Ladies and Gentlewomen* (1611), 188.
11. Hugh Platt, *Delightes for Ladies* (1603), G9^v.
12. Tuke, A4^v.
13. John Taylor, *Wit and Mirth* (1635), B6^v.
14. Tuke, 10.
15. Rich, *The Honestie of this Age*, 34.
16. Richard Brathwaite, *Ar't Asleep Husband? A Boulster Lecture* (1661), 313.
17. W. M., *The Queens Closet Opened* (1661), 115.
18. Francis Dickinson, *A Pretious Treasury of Twenty Rare Secrets* (1649), A4. This book and a similar one by Dickinson and Salvator Winters, both very rare, repeat some recipes.
19. *A Closet for Ladies and Gentlewomen* (1611), 188.
20. W. M., 146.
21. Platt, G9, G9^v.
22. Ibid., H3, H3^v.
23. *A Closet for Ladies and Gentlewomen*, 189.
24. Platt, G12.
25. Bulwer, 58, 62.
26. Dickinson, A4.
27. W. M., 100.
28. Bulwer, 78.

29. Quoted in Phillis Cunnington, *Medieval and Tudor Costume* (Boston: Plays, Inc., 1968), 52.

30. *The Book of Prittie Conceites* (1586?), A4^v.

31. W. M., 55.

32. C[hamberlain], T[homas], *The Compleat Midwifes Practice* (1656), 135.

33. Platt, H7^v.

34. Ibid., H10^v.

35. Dickinson, A3.

36. Juan Luis Vives, *The Instruction of a Christen Woman* (c.1529), H4^v. See also Mary Beth Rose, "Women in Men's Clothing" in *English Literary Renaissance* (Autumn 1984), 369.

37. David Cressy, paper read at the Huntington Library, San Marino, Calif., May 14, 1994.

38. Thomas Dawson, *The Good Huswifes Jewell* (1596), 52.

Chapter Eight

Conclusion

Conclusion

*I*n the Tudor-Stuart era English women were hidden in the shadow of the male world. Men dealt with the public arena, women with the more obscure private sector. Public activities—politics, wars, religious debates, legal matters—are all documented and discussed in print by male writers. The other half of life, the domestic part, is also represented in print, not by the women who lived and worked in the households, but by men. Men were the writers of record. They set down what they considered important. It seemed important to them to tell women how to live—the views of the women themselves were largely ignored.

Women and men who lived in this controlled society were wrapped in mores that differ vastly from those in practice near the year 2000. Political, religious and social rules created an environment that would be intolerable in the modern Western world. Equality, democracy, and universal education were nonexistent; in fact, the very concepts were barely nascent. Theirs was a realm that granted little or no power to the mass of the people, male or female. A distinct class structure separated and layered the citizenry. While a few men could vote, no women had that right. The Christian beliefs of the time elevated man above woman; these tenets were inculcated from birth. Patriarchy and a "natural" hierarchy substituted for equality, and the superiority of the male was enshrined in civil and ecclesiastical law. Most necessities of life were still

---

Opposite page:
ENGLISH GENTLEWOMAN, entire title page of *The Englsih Gentlewoman* by Richard Brathwaite (London, 1631). By permission of The Huntington Library, San Marino, Calif.

191

produced at home, so men and women usually worked in close proximity; male oversight was therefore fairly constant.

These wide gulfs between the culture of the Tudor-Stuart era and ours must be remembered during any reading of male-authored books of the time. Men cannot be condemned out of hand for instructing and directing women in every phase of their lives. They no doubt felt they were doing their Christian duty by upholding their natural role within the family. With all the domestic work, childbearing, and work for hire that women were expected to undertake, they were too overburdened and underprepared to protest publicly.

My contention is that *most* women lived within the broadest parameters set by society, though not in all particulars and not without occasional private protest. It is difficult to prove that most women would have elected their situation; it is likely, however, that most acceded to it.

No, women did not accept all directions. Nor did they abide by the rules all the time. Elaine Hobbey points out, in the introduction to her *Virtue of Necessity: English Women's Writing 1649–1688*, "The existence of [an] assertion suggests a need to assert it. It does not tell us much about whether readers then would have agreed with it."[1] Men asserted much, and repeatedly, suggesting a continuous need to hammer home their positions. Some women ignored the assertions and ventured out into worldly matters, taking errant relatives to court over property claims, fleeing impossible marriages, even speaking out occasionally or writing for publication. Others, deputized by their husbands, handled estates in the men's absence. We are hearing more and more of these strong women. Yet there were many more, like diarists Margaret Hoby and Alice Thornton, who found solace in their well-entrenched religious beliefs and appeared to accept their fate without question.

We must not forget the average woman, who didn't write or even read. Most lived with the situation as they found it. They raised their families, faced frequent and devastating losses of children, loved—or tolerated—their husbands (sometimes scolding and nagging to wriggle into a tolerable existence). Despite their occasional protests they lived in a world that said: (1) men are the leaders and superiors of women; (2) upon marriage, the man and woman "become one," with the woman assuming the passive role; (3) nearly all that is the woman's becomes the husband's to control after marriage; (4) women should not leave their domestic duties, except to attend church or when bidden by their husbands to do so; (5) women are under the care of fathers or husbands until widowed; (6) pregnancy from rape is the woman's fault; (7) women are the brunt of jokes in ninety-nine ballads for every one slanted against men; and (8) unmarried women rarely have independent incomes but must depend on the largesse of fathers or heirs.

Within this world, spelled out for females by authority figures, were their many domestic duties: preparing food and remedies, brewing, tending to the ill in the family, rearing children, dressing correctly, managing servants, and behaving with proper demeanor.

Most women were not educated, nor were they encouraged or even allowed to express themselves in a male-dominated society.[2] A few women wrote, though their work in many cases was criticized or ignored. Very few female-authored publications were popular enough to go into extra editions. Eleanor Davies, a prolific early female author (she self-published her work), found some of her manuscripts torn up by her disgusted husband. Margaret Tyler translated *The Mirrour of Princely Deedes and Knighthood*, the first book of a serial romance, yet never completed the series. Lady Mary Wroth wrote a romance, *The Countesse of Mountgomeries Urania*, in imitation of the popular *Arcadia*, by her uncle, Sir Philip Sidney, but it was highly criticized and never republished. Margaret Cavendish, the Duchess of Newcastle, was ridiculed for her varied outpouring of literature. *The Tragedy of Mariam*, the first drama by a woman playwright, Elizabeth, Lady Falkland, caused serious contention within the family and even estrangement from her husband, and was withdrawn from circulation.[3]

Women's writing sometimes mentioned the restrictions under which they struggled. Margaret Tyler argued that, since women read romances, they ought to be allowed to write or translate them as well. But her cry went largely unheard—or unread. Alice Thornton and Anne Clifford, whose journals went unpublished until long after their deaths, recorded often-lengthy disputes with male relatives over property and personal matters, whose outcomes usually reflected their powerlessness in the male-dominated society. The Willoughby family letters exemplify women's helplessness in a hateful marital situation. The wife, after bearing some one dozen children, left her husband. When she found she had no status without him she begged him to take her back. But he insisted that she agree to obey him henceforth without question before he would have her back. These anecdotes suggest that the society described in the male literature had a vivid reality outside of the books. Even Bathsua Makin's *Essay to Revive the Antient Education of Gentlewomen* made only a limited proposal: "My intention is not to equalize women to men, much less to make them superior. They are the weaker sex."[4] Katherine Philips, poet and Royalist, wrote about what she considered the outrageous murder of King Charles I, though she admitted that she would normally not be involved in such a matter since government and politics were out of a woman's realm. Underlying all these situations was the recognition, by the women writers, of their socially inferior position.

In the early decades of the seventeenth century, angry arguments over the good versus evil in women—known euphemistically as the "controversy over women"—appeared in print. The main antagonists were a man named Joseph Swetnam and several, mostly pseudonymous women who rebutted his uncomplimentary analysis of the female sex. But Swetnam's book, sarcastic in its ridicule, was by far the most popular and oft-reprinted of the group. Like the ballads, "controversy" literature was tilted pointedly against the female sex. For in literature, as in other public pursuits, it continued to be a man's world.

Other literature was occasionally complimentary about women—but the compliment was for behaving in the "proper" manner as prescribed by men. An example is *A Christal Glasse for Christian Women*, the short pamphlet by Philip Stubbes about his young wife's religious devotion. The booklet reconfirmed patriarchal attitudes, and its amazing popularity (well over two dozen printings) is evidence of interest in the conforming—not the independent—woman.

More private writings by women of the time are surfacing today. Other works, published in the sixteenth and seventeenth centuries, warrant careful reexamination as the position of women receives unprecedented attention. Still the fact remains that it was relatively rare for women to write in the Tudor-Stuart period. Few books, manuscripts, letters, essays, diaries, guidebooks, prayers or other written works by females survive, whereas a barrage of instructions, guidebooks, prayers, sermons, essays, jest books, fictional literature, ballads, advice books, and letters—all written by men—descend to us today.

Despite the evidence in women's writing that their lives were controlled and restricted, there is almost no sign that anyone argued against the oft-quoted Biblical pronouncements that women were subservient to men, that they were born to be helpmates to their husbands, and that men were to be in the leadership positions. A few writers admitted that women *could* have accomplished much and contributed intellectually to society had they been given the educational opportunities of men. For example, Daniel Tuvil wrote, early in the seventeenth century:

> The male shall not be thought more worthy than the female in regard of his essence because they be comprehended, both under one kind, but if in anything he have the start and advantage, it is merely by accident and no way else.[5]

And:

> It hath been our policy from the beginning to busy them in domestical affairs, thereby to divert them from more serious employments, in which if they had not surmounted us, they would at least have shown themselves our equals and our parallels.[6]

Agrippa, Edward More, and others also published books in defense of women. But these pro-female writings were but an eddy in a rushing river of criticism, advice, and instructions based on male superiority. Bathsua Makin herself saw education merely as an improvement on frivolous living, but not as serious preparation for accomplishment in the public arena.

Current scholarship sometimes concludes—perhaps wishfully— that women did *not*, in fact, act in accordance with the prescriptions given them. Scholars offer as proof published and unpublished works by a few women of the period (and legal wars over property) in which women protested the status quo. Historical records and literature portray occasional rebellious and non-conforming women. Other women, of necessity, stepped successfully into domestic and even community leadership roles while their men were away at war or in exile during the Civil War and Commonwealth period, and during the interregnum more women, particularly Quakers, expressed themselves in print. These women proved their ability to act and to write authoritatively in the male world, but for most it was a temporary change. Granted, by the eighteenth century more women were writing successfully and with less criticism. That was a definite step up. Yet the eighteenth century also saw a trivializing of women's place in society, particularly in court circles and the upper classes where women were seen as baby-making machines and playthings. Independence for most was still centuries away.

One other small step toward independence *did* take place in this period. A stream of women began moving, on their own, from village and country to London and other urban areas in search of better lives. Evidence of this migration appears prominently in contemporary fiction and drama. The influx of young women into the towns provided additional servants for town houses and tipped the sex ratio toward a larger female urban population, but it is questionable as to whether it raised the living standards of the girls.

Still, life for most women continued to follow a general rule of domesticity and subservience. The pressures to conform exerted their tidal pull. Economic circumstances, religious convictions, fear of social ostracism, even love and respect for their husbands were often enough to convince conformists and rebels alike to stay within the structure of their male-dominated world.

Descriptions of ideal behavior for women continued to pour from the presses. Men were repetitively insistent with the instructions they gave to women. No doubt men, too, believed what the established interpretations of the Bible told them: that it was their duty to instruct women, to limit them to household duties, and to insist on their chastity, silence, patience, submission, and general conformity.

It is also possible that men feared the opposite sex in ways unique to the times. There was a theory in Early Modern England that every sex act reduced the life of the man by one day by spilling part of his life-giving "seed." A lustful woman, then, could cause the early demise of a man. Thus it was wise to insist on chastity and one sex partner for women, not only to prevent cuckolding but to preserve men's lives. As for education: women would not—it was thought—act responsibly if given academic knowledge; therefore there was good reason to restrict such opportunities. Fear of witches, most of whom were female, was another reason to keep a close eye on women: insisting on godly behavior might help keep the devil at bay.

Men may also have felt threatened by wise, knowledgeable, and competent women. Better to keep them busy cooking, healing (in a limited way), sewing, and bearing babies than to let them compete with men. To this day the old expression "Keep them pregnant and don't buy them any shoes" is bandied about.

The Restoration not only returned the royal family to power, it also restored most women to more limited niches in society. Women of the aristocracy were now often seen as sex objects, married off young to produce heirs and otherwise considered little more than frivolous toys. Middle-class women, meanwhile, had acquired a small public voice during the Cromwell period, and by the last quarter of the seventeenth century more women were publishing. But their numbers were small and their words less brazen than their interregnum predecessors. The men had returned from war and life for women resumed its former restrictive state.

Religious belief was a major influence in women's lives. The Christian religion was the rock on which much of society stood. The church was one of the few places a proper woman could go outside of her home. It was also the place where sermons and homilies—required listening— repeated biblical fundamentals. And the Bible was cited as confirmation of what contemporary male writers were saying: women were the subservient sex. Churchmen repeated it. The more that women accepted this religious message, the more they would have to believe in their own inferiority. But there is no doubt that individual women drew much-needed strength from their religious convictions. Women's writing indicates that the message was accepted. Pious thoughts and prayers by women reinforced these beliefs. Almost all autobiographical writing by women makes repeated reference to their dependence on prayer, God's will, and the pronouncements of the (male) church hierarchy. Most women writers believed in careful religious upbringing. But the more they accepted the church and its teachings, the more they tightened their own bonds.

Much of what men advised and taught was deeply rooted in Christian beliefs. The superior position of men was not the only concept endorsed by Bible and man. The ideal woman, said both, would stay at home, serve her husband as a helper, concern herself primarily with domestic duties, dress and behave as the Bible taught, carefully guard her chastity, and avoid public activities or speech. Few women who expressed themselves on the matter in writing contradicted this.

Joan Larsen Klein, a modern feminist, suspects that actual life was different from "theological assumptions about woman's place." But she recognizes that "only an exceptional woman . . . was able to escape the restrictions that her father, her husband, and her society imposed upon her," and she hopes "that the profound silence of the large majority of women in the period does not necessarily reflect adversely upon either their private achievements or their private joys."[7] That is my position as well.

Women had assignments in life that most of them fulfilled reasonably well, if not joyfully. Perhaps more letters and journals will be found describing joyful lives for more of them. Unfortunately, current evidence suggests otherwise, especially in the upper classes, where early, arranged marriages boded ill for future happiness. Women who sought respectability, took their religious training seriously, and looked to books for guidance on how to handle household chores were largely of the middling sort. We know less about the mass of lower-class women: ballads, jest books, fiction, and the occasional journal entry about errant servants create the impression of a large body of women who flouted ideals, drank immoderately, talked incessantly, and lusted after men. Yet it is unfair to conclude that less fortunate women were more corrupt, largely on the evidence of fiction and jests. After the Restoration and the Puritans' loss of power in England, court histories suggest a breakdown of sexual morals at the highest levels of society. King Charles II led the way with his avid appetite for women. Immorality, then, was hardly exclusive to the lower classes.

Much evidence of a patronizing manner toward women writers can be found. There was the man who explained that he was merely putting the recipes of a woman in good order for publication (implying they were in a mess to begin with). The earliest dictionaries were addressed to women "and other untutored persons." One gentleman recommended a simple handwriting style for women, reasoning they would find more complicated types too difficult. When women wrote pious thoughts, prayers, and religious guides for their children, their writing was tolerated; when they joined in intellectual topics, they were criticized.

The last quarter of the twentieth century has brought forth a female Renaissance. To understand why women's creativity was dampened or hidden during the original Renaissance while that of men began to emerge, it is vital to know the obstacles between women and their writing, publishing, and even thinking in creative terms in that first Renaissance.

New scholarship will alter our views of Early Modern Englishwomen. We can hope their lives will prove to have been more vigorous and less docile than present evidence indicates. After all, they had broad responsibilities in what was still a domestic economy. It might be inspiring to learn that, by and large, those women were in a continual state of enlightened protest. But it is more likely that they were not, and that most of the major efforts toward women's independence were undertaken much later in history. ❧

Notes

1. Elaine Hobby, *Virtue of Necessity: English Women's Writing 1649–1688* (London: Virago Press, 1988), 2.
2. Estimates vary, though scarcely 1 percent of all writing published in the period being discussed here (1525–1675) was by women. See Hobby, 6.
3. Retha M. Warnicke, *Women of the English Renaissance and Reformation* (Westport, Conn.: Greenwood Press, 1983), 189–91.
4. Bathsua Makin, *An Essay to Revive the Antient Education of Gentlewomen* (1673), 29. See Hobby, 200–203, for an analysis of Makin's writing.
5. Daniel Tuvil, *Asylum Veneris or a Sanctuary for Ladies: Justly Protecting Them, Their Virtues and Sufficiencies from the Foule Aspersons and Forged Imputations of Traducing Spirits.* (1616), 140.
6. Ibid., 100.
7. Joan Larsen Klein, *Daughters, Wives and Widows: Writings by Men About Women and Marriage in England 1500–1640* (Urbana and Chicago: Univ. of Ill. Press, 1992), xii–xiii.

Bibliography

Bibliography

$\mathcal{E}$ ntries in bold type are sixteenth- or seventeenth-century works, first published in the year shown. The place of publication is London unless otherwise noted. Either the Pollard and Redgrave or the Wing *Short-Title Catalogue* (see below) will indicate where copies of the books can be found. Entries in regular type are reference books including those that print abridgements or excerpts of the early works. Also included in regular type are manuscripts dating from the Early Modern period but published for the first time in later centuries. Multiple editions of books published through 1700 are indicated with one asterisk for two to nine editions; two asterisks for ten or more.

A. *The Passoinate* [passionate]*Morrice.* 1593. Reprint in The New Shakespeare Society, Series VI, 2. Edited by Frederick J. Furnivall. London: Trubner, 1876.

Discusses intermarriage between classes.

Agrippa, Henricus Cornelius. *Female Pre-eminence or the Dignity and Excellence of that Sex Above the Male.* 1670.

Translation and adaptation of original translation of Agrippa's *A Treatise of the Nobilitie of Woman Kynde* (1542 and 1553). Strong advocate of women's abilities in all fields including military and legal. Refutes Saint Paul's admonition that women were only subservient to men by citing other biblical instances of great leadership and judgment by women.

Opposite page:
MAN WRITING AT DESK, frontispiece of *The Treasurie of Commodious Conceits* by John Partridge (London, 1573). By permission of The Huntington Library, San Marino, Calif.

Allestree, Richard. *The Ladies Calling.* Oxford: 1673.**
Allestree also wrote *The Gentlemans Calling.* Each is a guide to proper living.

[Armstrong, Archibald]. *A Banquet of Jests.* 1630.*

Attending to Women in Early Modern England. Edited by Betty S. Travitsky and Adele F. Seeff. Newark: Univ. of Delaware Press; London and Toronto: Association Univ. Presses, 1994.
Papers from symposium of the same name held Nov. 8–10, 1990, at the University of Maryland at College Park.

Aveling, James Hobson. *English Midwives: Their History and Prospects.* London: Hugh K. Elliott, 1967.
Reprint of original 1872 edition. Favored midwives' education and their use in normal deliveries but did not think them capable of handling emergencies.

B., M. *The Ladies Cabinet Enlarged and Opened.* 1654.*
General household guide similar to *The Ladies Cabinet Opened,* 1639.

B., Ste. *Counsel to the Husband; To the Wife Instruction.* 1608.
Marriage sermon.

Baer, Karl Ernst, von. *De Ovi Mammalium et Homini Genesi.* Leipzig, 1827.
Forty-page (Latin) letter setting forth von Baer's theory of ovulation. Led to first correct understanding of conception.

Bayly, Lewis, Bp. *The Practise of Pietie.* 1612.**
Extremely popular (around 100 editions in England and elsewhere) guide to Christian duties; most were thick, pocket-size 12° publications. Meditations and prayers used also for instructing children.

Becon, Thomas. *Workes.* 1560–1564 or *see* 1844 edition of his *The Catachism.* Cambridge: Univ. Press, 1844.
Part I includes extensive instructions for raising young girls.

Bentley, Thomas. *The Monument of Matrones.* 1582.
Large book of prayers for and by women plus female biographies and religious thoughts.

Besant, Sir Walter. *London in the Time of the Stuarts.* London: Adam & Charles Black, 1903.

Billingsley, Martin. *The Pens Excellencie or the Secretaries Delighte.* [1617?]*
Guide to penmanship. Includes remarks about female writing and its value.

Block, Ruth R. "Untangling the Roots of Modern Sex Roles: A Survey of Four Centuries of Change." *Signs*. 4:237–52.
> Discusses contrasting sexual appetites of men and women as perceived in different centuries; changing status of midwives in England, Europe, and America.

Boke of Kervynge [Carving], *Here Begynneth the*. 1508.
> Starts off with the "Terms of a Carver," e.g. "Lift that swan, Spoil that hare." Includes duties of carver, chamberlain, butler, the order of precedence (Pope at top) and sauces for various meat, fish, and fowl. A guide for a royal household.

Booke of Cookerie, A, and the Order of Meats to bee Served to the Table . . . . *1620*.

Booke of Cookerie, A, Otherwise called The Good Huswives Handmaid for the Kitchin. 1594.

[Book of Cookery] *See* several books known by this or similar name.

Book of Fruits and Flowers Shewing the Nature and Use of Them, either for Meat or Medicine, A. 1653.
> Illustrated book of food and remedy recipes.

Booke of Prittie Conceites, The. [1586?].*
> Early book of miscellaneous household and cosmetic hints.

Booke of Soveraigne Approved Medicines and Remedies, A. 1577.
> Household remedies including many for childbearing women.

Borde, Andrew. . . . *A Dyetary of Helthe*. [1542].*
> Considered first physician to write in English, according to O'Malley (*see*).

Border, Daniel. *The English Unparalell'd Physitian and Churirgian*. 1651.

Bornstein, Diane. *Distaves and Dames: Renaissance Treatises for and about Women*. Delmar, N.Y.: Scholars' Facsimiles & Reprints, 1978.
> Reprints *The Gospelles of Dystaves, The Northern Mothers Blessing, The Boke of the Cyte of Ladies, The Instruction of a Christen Woman*.

Brathwaite, Richard. *Ar't Asleepe Husband? A Boulster Lecture*. 1640.*
> Jest book. Frontispiece of wife disturbing husband's sleep by talking.

Brears, Peter, Maggie Black, Gill Corbishley, Jane Renfrew and Jennifer Stead. *A Taste of History: 10,000 Years of Food in Britain*. London: English Heritage/British Museum Press. 1993.
> Pages 137–215 summarize Tudor-Stuart cooking; includes descriptions of utensils.

Bruto, Giovanni Michele. *The Necessarie, Fit, and Convenient Education of a Yong Gentlewoman.* 1598.

Severely restrictive. *See* Salter for another translation.

Bullinger, Heinrich. *The Christen State of Matrimony.* [Antwerp, 1541].

Bulwer, John. *Anthropometamorphosis.* 1653.*

Describes and laments extremes in clothing.

Buttes, Henry. *Dyets Dry Dinner.* 1599.

Each opening discusses one food; its use on one page, stories about it for "table-talk" on other. Dry dinner is without wine "except Tabacco (which also is but Dry Drinke)."

C., T. [C., R. in later editions] *The Complete Midwifes Practice.* 1656.*

Based on 1609 book by Louise Bourgeois, midwife to the French queen.

Camden, Carroll. *The Elizabethan Woman.* Houston, New York, and London: Elsevier Press, 1952.

Good early study including discussion of female authors (page 58) and household skills essential for girls to learn.

Campbell, Mildred. *The English Yeoman Under Elizabeth and the Early Stuarts.* New York: Augustus M. Kelley, 1968.

Carter, Thomas. *Carters Christian Commonwealth or Domesticall Dutyes Deciphered.* 1627.

Carter was an advocate of severe discipline and corporal punishment. His book is divided, as are many family guides, into sections on the duties of husbands, wives, children, masters, and servants.

Castiglione, Baldassare. *The Courtyer of Count Baldessar Castilio . . . done into Englyshe by Thomas Hoby.* 1561.** Reprint in *The Tudor Translations,* Vol. 23, edited by W. E. Henley. London: David Nutt, 1900.

Courtesy guide for noble and court circles.

Cawdrey, Robert. *A Table Alphabeticall . . . Gathered for the Benefit and Helpe of Ladies, Gentlewomen, or Any Other Unskillfull Persons.* 1604.*

First English-English dictionary.

[C]hamberlain, [T]homas. *The Complete Midwifes Practice Enlarged . . .* 1656.*

Based on French work on obstetrics by Louise Boursier (or Bourgeois), "late midwife to the Queen of France," who is pictured on frontispiece. Some suggestions for care of babies mixed in with guidance on birthing and care of the mother.

Clark, Alice. *Working Life of Women in the Seventeenth Century.* London and
New York: Routledge, 1992. First edition 1919.

Valuable overall discussion of women with new introduction and extensive bibliography.

Cleaver, Robert. *A Codly* [godly]*Form of Householde Governement.* 1598.

Clifford, Anne, Countess of Dorset, Pembroke, and Montgomery. 1590–1676.
The Diaries of Lady Anne Clifford. Edited by D. J. H. Clifford. Stroud,
Glos: Alan Sutton,1990; Wolfeboro Falls, N.H.: Alan Sutton, 1991.

Not printed until three centuries after she wrote. This edition incorporates all of
her writings. *See also* George Williamson's detailed life of Lady Anne and her
Diary, edited by Vita Sackville-West. London: William Heinemann, 1924.

Clinton, Elizabeth, Countess of Lincoln. *The Countess of Lincoln's Nurserie.* 1622.

Short but strong recommendation to mothers to nurse their own children, by a
mother of eighteen.

Closet for Ladies and Gentlewomen, A. 1608.**

Popular, pocket-size recipe book, mostly medicinal; decorative border. Somewhat
different format in later editions.

Copeman, W. S. C. *Doctors and Disease in Tudor Times.* London: Dawson's of
Pall Mall, 1960.

Helpful analyses of relations among physicians, surgeons, and untutored healers
including women.

Court of Good Counsell, The. 1607.

Long title continues, "Wherein is set downe the true rules, how a man should
choose a good wife from a bad, and a woman a good husband from a bad.
Wherein is also expressed, the great care that parents should have, for the bestowing of their children in mariage: And likewise how children ought to behave
themselves towardes their parents."

Crawford, Patricia. "Women's Published Writings 1600–1700." *Women in
English Society 1500–1800.* Edited by Mary Prior. London: Methuen, 1985.

Excellent bibliography.

Cressy, David. *Literacy and the Social Order: Reading and Writing in Tudor and
Stuart England.* Cambridge: Univ. Press, 1980.

Court records used to reveal percentage of city and country men and women
who can write their own names.

_____. "Literacy in Pre-Industrial England." *Societas—A Review of Social History*. Summer 1974. 4:229–40.

Information on literacy in Early Modern England.

Crouch, Humphrey. *Loves Court of Conscience . . . Whereunto is Annexed a Kinde Husband's Advise to His Wife.* 1637. Reprint in *Illustrations of Old English Literature*. Edited by J. Payne Collier. London: Privately Printed, 1866.

Crouch was a voluminous ballad writer. This is the rhymed complaint of a man who claims he loves his wife and feels wealthy because he has children but who suffers from a talkative and disobedient wife. Advice is to love, be silent, and be obedient.

Crowley, Robert. *The Voyce of the Laste Trumpet.* 1549.*

Rhymed description of twelve classes of men, one of which is women.

Culpeper, Nicholas. *A Directory for Midwives.* 1651.**

Very popular self-help guide for women and midwives. Includes short section at end, "A Tractate of the Cure of Infants." Greatly abridged edition, *Culpeper's Book of Birth: A Seventeenth Century Guide to Having Lusty Children*, edited by Ian Thomas. Exeter: Webb & Bower, 1985.

_____. *The English Physitian: or An Astrologo-Physical Discourse of the Vulgar Herbs of this Nation.* 1652.

This is the popular herbal for which Culpeper was particularly known. Each herb is described and then its uses noted. Sometimes referred to as Culpeper's herbal.

Cunnington, Phillis. *Medieval and Tudor Costume. Boston: Plays, Inc., 1968.*

Short text with black-and-white illustrations and explanations of clothing terms.

Cunnington, C. Willett and Phillis. *Handbook of English Costume in the Seventeenth Century.* London: Faber and Faber, 1955, 1972.

Daughters, Wives, and Widows: Writings by Men about Women and Marriage in England: 1500–1640. Edited by Joan Larsen Klein. Urbana and Chicago: Univ. of Illinois Press, 1992.

Includes wording of the marriage ceremony from 1559 *Book of Common Prayer*; excerpts from 1563 *Homily of the State of Matrimony*; *Lawes Resolutions of Women's Rights*, and books (*see* their entries) by Erasmus, Vives, Stubbes, Perkins, Roesslin, Tusser, Brathwaite, DuBosc, Leigh.

Dawson, Thomas. *The Good Huswifes Jewell.* 1587.*

General recipe book with small section on husbandry; 1610 edition has interesting illustration of women in various housewifely roles.

DeMolen, Richard L. *See* Mulcaster.

Dickinson, Francis [Francisco]. *A Pretious Treasury of Twenty Rare Secrets.* 1649.

One of several remedy books published in 1649 with similar titles. Dickinson is coauthor of *A Pretious Treasury or a New Dispensatory*, published in same year.

Digby, Kenelm, Sir. *Choice and Experimented Receipts in Physick and Chirurgery.* 1668.*

Published posthumously. Digby was many things: a Catholic, sometimes a Protestant, confident of Cromwell, Royalist, foreign representative, alchemist, and quack.

Discourses of Sexuality from Aristotle to AIDS. Edited by Domna C. Stanton. Ann Arbor: Univ. of Michigan Press, 1992.

Fourteen wide-ranging essays. See especially Part One, "The History of Sexuality."

Drummond, J. C. and A. Wilbraham. *The Englishman's Food: A History of five Centuries of English Diet.* 2nd ed. London: Jonathan Cope, 1958.

Intertwines medical beliefs with discussion of foods for all classes. *See also* Hartley.

DuBosc, Jacques. *The Compleat Woman.* 1639.

French guide recommending education for women who should be able to participate, like men, in public affairs.

E., T. *The Lawes Resolutions of Womens Rights: or The Lawes Provision for Women.* 1632. Facsimile reprint. New York: Garland, 1978.

Narrative summaries of laws pertaining to women. *See* Joan Larsen Klein's *Daughters, Wives, and Widows* for excerpts (entry appears in this bibliography under its title).

Emerson, Kathy Lynn. *Wives and Daughters: The Women of Sixteenth-Century England.* Troy, N.Y.: Whitson, 1984.

Biographical bibliography of prominent women; also of men with whom women were affiliated.

Epulario, or, The Italian Banquet. 1598.

Translation of 1516 Italian book by Giovanne de Rosselli. Includes some exotic recipes.

Erasmus, Desiderus. *A Devout Treatise Upon the Pater Noster.* Translated by Margaret More Roper. [1526?]*

Short introduction by Richard Hyrde is early statement on female education originating in English language. Frontispiece shows woman at desk.

_____. *A Lytell Booke of Good Maners for Chyldren.* 1532.*
Practical guide to etiquette with emphasis on table manners for boys. Printed in columns, one Latin, one English.

Ezell, Margaret J. M. *The Patriarch's Wife: Literary Evidence and the History of the Family.* Chapel Hill and London: Univ. of North Carolina Press, 1987.
Discusses the gap between theory and practice in a patriarchal society. Appendices include transcriptions of three essays on women's rights and virtues.

Fenner, Dudley. *The Order of Householde.* 1584.
Government of the family based closely on biblical references. Tiny print font.

Ferguson, Moira. *First Feminists: British Women Writers 1578–1799.*
Excerpts from twenty-eight early writers who advocated women's rights.

Fontanus, Nicholas. *The Womans Doctour: or an Exact and Distinct Explanation of all such Diseases as are Peculiar to that Sex.* 1652.
Translation. See pages 128–37 for discussion of barrenness.

Forbes, Thomas R. "By What Disease or Casualty: The Changing Face of Death in London." *Health, Medicine and Mortality in the Sixteenth Century.* Cambridge: Univ. Press, 1979. 117–39.

Foxe, John. *Actes and Monuments.* aka *The Book of Martyrs.* 1563.*
Huge, popular, pulpit-size book. Many illustrations of martyrs burning including one of three women and a baby.

Fraser, Antonia. *The Weaker Sex.* New York: Knopf, 1984.
Lengthy and useful analysis of women in seventeenth century, using largely female writing for descriptions.

Friedman, Alice T. "Portrait of a Marriage: The Willoughby Letters of 1565–1586." *Signs.* Spring 1986. 11:542–55.
Describes miserable marriage and how wife had no power without her husband.

Fussell, G. E. and K. R. *The English Countrywoman: A Farmhouse Social History A. D. 1500–1900.* London: Andrew Melrose, 1953.
With companion volume, *The Farmer's Tools A.D. 1500–1900*, it provides good early look at separate duties of working men and women.

Gardiner, Dorothy Kempe. *English Girlhood at School: A Study of Women's Education Through Twelve Centuries.* Oxford: Univ. Press, 1929.
Good history of female schools including the earliest in seventeenth century.

Gataker, Thomas. *A Good Wife Gods Gift.* 1620.*
Includes marriage duties.

Germin [Jermin], Michael. *Paraphrastical Meditation.* 1638.
Ends with description of virtuous woman.

Gibbon, Charles. *A Work Worth Reading . . . .* 1591.
Dialogue using constant biblical references. Includes how to bestow children in marriage and disinheritance.

Gillis, John R. *For Better, For Worse: British Marriages, 1600 to the Present.* New York: Oxford Univ. Press, 1985.
Good for wedding customs that differed over the years.

Goeurot, Jehan. *See* Thomas Phaer, tr.

Goreau, Angeline, *The Whole Duty of a Woman: Female Writers in Seventeenth Century England.* Garden City, N.Y.: Dial Press, 1985.
Sections of many feminist texts and some of the male writing that inspired them.

Gouge, William. *Of Domesticall Duties.* 1622.*
Lengthy marriage guide.

Goulianos, Joan. *By a Woman Writt: Literature from Six Centuries by and about Women.* Indianapolis and New York: Bobbs-Merrill, 1973.
Includes selections from women authors Margery Kemp, Jane Anger, Alice Thornton, Aphra Behn, Anne Finch, Margaret Cavendish.

Great Britain, Public Record Office. *Letters and Papers, Foreign and Domestic of the Reign of Henry VIII.* Edited by J. S. Brewer, R. H. Brodie, James Gairdner. 21 vols., 1862–1910. Reprinted by Kraus Reprint, Ltd. 1965.
See Vol. 8, page 101, for reference to Henry VIII's opinion on duty owed by daughter to father over mother.

Grey, Elizabeth, Countess of Kent. *A Choice Manual or Rare and Select Secrets in Physick and Chyrurgery.* 1653.**
Published posthumously. Editor William Jarvis claimed pocket-size book of medical remedies, preserving, conserving, and candying recipes was collected by the Countess.

————. *A True Gentlewomans Delight.* 1653.*
One of two books purported to be by the Countess but published posthumously.

Grymeston, Elizabeth. *Miscelanea. Meditations. Memoratives.* 1604.
Devotional-instructional guide for Grymeston's only surviving son.

Guibert, Philibert. *The Charitable Physitian with the Charitable Apothe-cary.* 1639.*
Translation of French doctor's work. Includes information on specific medicines.

Guillemeau, James, *Child-birth or, the Happy Deliverie of Women. Wherein is Set Downe the Government of Women in the Time of their Breeding Childe: of their Travaile, both Naturall, and Contrary to Nature . . . .* 1612*
Midwifery book translated from the French. Includes "The Nursing of Children" and some illustrations of fetus in womb.

Guthrie, Douglas. *A History of Medicine.* London: Thomas Nelson, 1958.
Seventeenth century described as time of "intense intellectual activity" but a continuation of old medical methods.

Guttentag, Marcia and Paul F. Secord. *Too Many Women? The Sex Ratio Question.* Beverly Hills, London, New Delhi: Sage Publications, 1983.

Hake, Edward. *A Compendious Fourme of Education.* Bound with *A Touchstone for this Time Present.* 1574.
Opposed to dancing, painting, unseemly clothing; "I would to God that maids at the least wise might be brought up, if not in learning, yet in honest trades and occupation." (C5)

Hannay, Patrick. *A Happy Husband or, Directions for a Maide to Choose her Mate.* 1619.
Marriage guide; Brathwaite's twelve-page *The Good Wife* is appended.

Hartley, Dorothy. *Food in England.* 2nd ed. London: Macdonald, 1979.
Social history of foods; includes drawings of utensils. *See also* Drummond and Wilbraham.

Health, Medicine and Mortality in the Sixteenth Century. Edited by Charles Webster. Cambridge: Univ. Press, 1979.

Henderson, Katherine Usher and Barbara F. McManus. *Half Humankind: Contexts and Texts of the Controversy about Women in England, 1540–1640.* Urbana and Chicago: Univ. of Illinois Press, 1985.
Includes selections from the major publications (by both men and women) on the controversy over women, plus bibliography.

Herman, Judith and Marguerite Shalett Herman. *The Cornucopia; Being a Kitchen Entertainment and Cookbook . . . . 1390–1899*. New York: Harper & Row, 1973.
Many early recipes with explanations and commentary about them and food culture.

Heywood, Thomas. *A Curtaine Lecture.* 1637.*
Facetious marriage guide.

Hobby, Elaine. *Virtue of Necessity: English Women's Writing 1649–88*. London: Virago Press, 1988.
Helpful chapters on "Skills Books—Housewifery, Medicine, Midwifery" and "Education."

Hogrefe, Pearl. *Tudor Women: Commoners and Queens*. Ames, Iowa: Iowa State Univ. Press, 1975.
Discusses limitations on women and nonconforming activities of some.

Hornbeak, Katherine Gee. *The Complete Letter-Writer*. Northampton, Mass.: Smith College, 1934.
History of model letter-writing books with samples from several centuries.

Horowitz, Maryanne Cline. "Aristotle and Woman." *Journal of the History of Biology*. Fall 1976. 9:183–213.
Detailed analysis of Aristotle's theory that female is imperfect male incapable of public roles, and subject always to rule by superior male.

_____. "The 'Science' of Embryology Before the Discovery of the Ovum." *Connecting Spheres: Women in the Western World 1500 to the Present*. Edited by Marilyn Boxer and Jean Quataert. New York: Oxford Univ. Press, 1987.
See for Aristotelian idea of human generation.

Hughes, P. F. and J. F. Larkin. *Tudor Royal Proclamations*. New Haven: Yale Univ. Press, 1969.
Includes apparel ordinances.

Hull, Suzanne W. *Chaste, Silent & Obedient: English Books for Women 1475–1640*. San Marino, Calif: Huntington Library Press, 1982, 1988.
Includes bibliography and argument that enough women knew how to read to support stream of books directed to them.

Hyrde, Richard. *See* Erasmus.

Ingram, Martin. *Church Courts, Sex and Marriage in England 1570–1640.* Cambridge and New York: Cambridge Univ. Press, 1987.
   See page 219 for estimate on the number of pregnant brides.

Jinner, Sarah. *An Almanack or Prognostication.* 1658 to 1664.
   Also published as *The Womans Almanack.* Issues include medical cures, female sexual difficulties, prophecies. *See* Hobby, pages 181–82, for discussion of Jinner.

Joceline, Elizabeth. *The Mothers Legacie to Her Unborne Child.* 1624.*
   One of three moral and religious guides written in the early seventeenth century by mothers for their children. *See also* Leigh and Grymeston.

Jones of Hatton Garden. *His Book of Cures.* 1673.
   Example of self-advertising by a healer.

Josselin, The Rev. Ralph. *The Diary of . . .1616–1683.* London: Office of the [Camden] Society, 1908.
   Interesting collection of entries covering personal life and family, political developments, costs of household items, and teaching. Josselin was not a rich man.

K., T. *The Kitchen Physician: Or, a Guide for Good Housewives in Maintaining Their Families in Health . . . by T. K. Doctor in Physick.* 1680.
   A professional doctor who admitted that housewives and other untrained healers were capable of handling uncomplicated medical problems, and who shared some doctors' secrets and hints with them.

Kelly, Joan. "Early Feminist Theory and the Querelle des Femmes, 1400–1789." *Signs.* Autumn 1982. Vol. 8, No. 1.
   History of intellectual controversy over women as background of later women's movements. See page 7 for her belief that aristocratic women lost power as new class of domesticated women arose.

King, Margaret L. *Women of the Renaissance.* Chicago: Univ. Press, 1991.
   Part of series edited by Catharine R. Simpson, *Women in Culture and Society.* Includes Western Europe and England.

Knox, John. *The First Blast of the Trumpet Against the Monstrous Regiment* [Rule] *of Women.* Geneva, 1558.
   Diatribe against Catholic queens, which created problems for Knox when Protestant Elizabeth succeeded to throne in England.

Ladies Cabinet Opened, The. 1639.
   General household guide. Some recipes identical to M. B., *The Ladies Cabinet Enlarged and Opened,* 1654, though different pagination.

La Primaudaye, Peter de. *The French Academie.* 1586.*
How-to-live guide with section on duties of wives to their husbands.

Laqueur, Thomas. "Orgasm, Generation, and the Politics of Reproductive Biology." *Representations.* Berkeley: Univ. of California Press, Spring 1986.
Excellent technical history of misconceptions in a special issue with other articles on "Sexuality and the Social Body in the Nineteenth Century."

_____. *Making Sex: Body and Gender from the Greeks to Freud.* Cambridge, Mass.: Harvard Univ. Press, 1992.
Story of sex in western world from antiquity to present.

Laslett, Peter. *The World We Have Lost.* New York: Scribner, 1966.
See second edition, 1971, pages 32–33, for Gregory King's population statistics for 1688, and page 38 for chart and description of titles and ranks in Stuart England.

Laver, James. *Costume and Fashion: A Concise History.* New York: Oxford Univ. Press, 1983.

Leigh, Dorothy. *The Mothers Blessing: or the Godly Counsaile of a Gentle-Woman.* 1616.**
Advice for both boys and girls based on biblical verses.

Lerner, Gerda. *The Majority Finds Its Past.* New York: Oxford Univ. Press, 1979.

Lisle Letters, The: An Abridgement. Edited by Muriel St. Clare Byrne. Chicago: Univ. Press, 1983.
Letters of large, noble family during 1530s.

Lodge, Thomas. *A Treatise of the Plague.* 1603.
Lodge became a professional physician after a career as a prolific poet and playwright.

Lovejoy, A. O. *The Great Chain of Being.* Cambridge: Harvard Univ. Press, 1936.
Discusses concept of hierarchy.

M., W. *The Queens Closet Opened: Incomparable Secrets in Physick . . . which were Presented unto the Queen.* 1655.**
Very popular (seventeen editions to 1700).

_____. *The Compleat Cook . . . for Dressing of Flesh, and Fish, Ordering of Sauces, or Making of Pastry.* 1655.**
Recipes using very large quantities, perhaps to be made for large establishments or to intrigue those in lesser houses.

Macfarlane, Alan. *The Origins of English Individualism: The Family, Property and Social Transition.* Oxford: Basil Blackwell, 1978.
Includes views of marriage, peasantry to lower gentry.

McLaren, Angus. *A History of Contraception From Antiquity to the Present Day.* Oxford, Eng., and Cambridge, Mass.: Blackwell, 1990.
See especially pages 101–77.

_____. *Reproductive Rituals: The Perception of Fertility in England from the Sixteenth to the Nineteenth Century.* London and New York: Methuen, 1984.
Good for history of procreation theories and social implications of sex misconceptions. Considerable discussion of contraception as practiced in Early Modern England.

Maclean, Ian. *The Renaissance Notion of Woman: A Study in the Fortunes of Scholasticism and Medical Science in European Intellectual Life.* Cambridge: Univ. Press, 1980.
Erudite thesis. Includes summaries of classical theories of conception.

McMurtry, Jo. *Understanding Shakespeare's England.* Hamden, Conn.: Archon Books, 1989.
Brief explanations of every facet of Elizabethan life: money, marriage, music, and so on.

MacNalty, Sir Arthur Salisbury. *The Renaissance and its Influence on English Medicine, Surgery and Public Health. . . Being the Thomas Vicary Lecture for 1945.* London: C. Johnson [1946].

Makin, Bathsua. *An Essay to Revive the Antient Education of Gentlewomen.* 1673.
Appeal for female education by a woman.

Markham, Gervase. *The English House-wife.* 1631.** First printed in Markham's *Country Contentments.* 1615.

Includes directions for "Physicke, surgery, cookery, extraction of oyles, banqueting stuffe, ordering of great feasts, preserving of all sorts of wines, conceited secrets, distillations, perfumes, ordering of wooll, hempe, flax, making cloth, and dying, the knowledge of dayries, office of malting, of oates, their excellent uses in a family, of brewing, baking, and all other things belonging to an houshold." In other words, an extensive guide—and very popular.

Masek, Rosemary. "Women in an Age of Transition." *The Women of England from Anglo-Saxon Times to the Present.* Edited by Barbara Kanner. Hamden, Conn.: Archon Books, 1979.

Mauriceau, François. *The Accomplisht Midwife.* 1673. *

———. *The Diseases of Women with Child.* 1672.*

May, Robert. *The Accomplisht Cook or the Art and Mystery of Cookery.* 1660.*

Starts by repeating the terms of carving and how to carve each dish. Includes recipes for making mead and metheglin.

Merchant, Carolyn. *The Death of Nature: Women, Ecology, and the Scientific Revolution.* San Francisco: Harper & Row, 1980.

See especially Chapter 6, pages 149–65, "Production, Reproduction and the Female."

Meres, Francis. *Gods Arithmeticke.* 1597.

Marriage advice telling women to obey, honor, love, have patience, and be humble toward husbands on earth so they might find equality and honor in heaven.

Meyerowitz, Joanne. "Beyond the Feminine Mystique: A Reassessment of Postwar Mass Culture 1946–1958." *Journal of American History*, Vol. 79, 4: 1455-82.

Analyzes women's magazines concluding they were written more by women than men after World War II, contrary to prewar situation when articles specialized in housewives' interests, romantic fiction, marriage advice, recipes, fashions, and ads for household products, but also spotlighted women of achievement.

Milton, John. *The Doctrine and Discipline of Divorce.* 1643.* Reprint in *Complete Prose Works.* New Haven: Yale Univ. Press, 1959. Vol. 2: 217–356. Also in *John Milton: Selected Prose.* Edited by C. A. Patrides. Columbia: Univ. of Missouri Press, 1985. 112–80. Also in *Complete Poems and Major Prose.* Edited by Merritt Y. Hughes. New York: The Odyssey Press, 1957. Vol. II.

_____. *Tetrachordon*. 1645. Reprint in *Complete Prose Works*. New Haven: Yale Univ. Press, 1959. Vol. 2: 571–718.
Third of Milton's divorce pamphlets.

More, Edward. *A Lytle and Bryefe Treatys Called The Defence of Women and Especially of Englyshe Women Against the Schole Howse of Women.* [1560].
Short "defense" in rhyme. Supports women in relatively minor accusations, e.g. arranging of hair, wearing of foreign styles. Blames criticisms of women on men who do similar things without disappoval.

Morse, H. K. *Elizabethan Pageantry: A Pictorial Survey of Costume and its Commentators from 1560–1620.* London and New York: The Studio, 1934.
English and continental portraits with quotes and glossary.

Muffett [Moffet], Thomas. *Healths Improvement: or, Rules Comprizing and Discovering the Nature, Method, and Manner of Preparing all Sorts of Food Used in this Nation.* 1655.
Describes good diets, air, and various kinds of food.

Mulcaster, Richard. *Positions . . . for the Training up of Children.* 1581. Abridged edition, edited by Richard L. DeMolen. New York: Teachers College Press, 1971.
Prominent sixteenth-century schoolmaster discusses education for both girls and boys.

Munda, Constantia [pseud.]. *The Worming of a Mad Dog.* 1617.
Response to Swetnam. *See* Henderson and McManus for partial text and precis.

Murrell, John. *A Delightful Daily Exercise for Ladies and Gentlewomen.* 1621.
One of four cookbooks published by Murrell. This one has many candy recipes.

Nendick, Humphrey. *A Compendium of the Vertues Operations and Use of that applauded Antipancronicon called Nendick's Popular Pill.* 1674.
Another charlatan with a cure-all pill. This little leaflet tells where they are sold.

Norris, Herbert. *Costume and Fashion.* London: J. M. Dent, 1938.
Summarizes lives and clothing of leading members of royal families of France, England, Scotland, 1485–1603.

Office of Christian Parents Shewing How Children are to be Governed Throughout all Ages and Times of their Life. 1616.
Much on religious training; some specifics on raising daughters.

O'Malley, C. D. "Tudor Medicine and Biology." *The Huntington Library Quarterly*. San Marino, Calif.: Huntington Library Press, 1968–69. Vol. 32: 1–27.
Good summary of early medical books including midwifery.

Ortunez de Calahorra, Diego. *The Mirrour of Princely Deedes and Knighthood.* 1573. Translated by Margaret Tyler.

Oxford, Arnold Whitaker. *English Cookery Books to the Year 1850.* London: Oxford Univ. Press, 1913.
Early but useful bibliography. Cookbooks are listed by title, not author/title. Some annotations including reference to remedies in Digby's book [*see*] as "more filthy and superstitious than those of any preceding books" (p.34).

Oxinden Letters, The. Edited by Dorothy Gardiner. London: Constable, 1933.
Covers 1607–1642. Example of husband deputizing wife with detailed instructions to handle their estate (pp. 129–30); marriage arrangements (pp. 236–40).

———. Edited by Dorothy Gardiner. London: Sheldon, 1937.
Covers 1642–1670.

Paradise of Women: Writings by Englishwomen of the Renaissance. Edited by Betty Travitsky. Westport, Conn.: Greenwood Press, 1981.
See pages 3–13 for good short summary of women writers and their culturally imposed restraints; bibliography of women's writing pages 265–73. Claims women composed or translated more than 100 works from 1500 to 1640.

Partridge, John. *The Treasurie of Commodious Conceits, and Hidden Secrets.* 1573.**
Pocket-size book of household recipes. Book is addressed to women; frontispiece shows man at desk writing. *See Treasury of Hidden Secrets.*

Perkins, William. *Christian Economy or a Short Survey of the Right Manner of Erecting and Ordering a Family According to the Scriptures.* 1609.**
Reprints in his *Works.*
Translation from Latin. Famous and prolific Puritan writer. *See Daughters, Wives, and Widows* for excerpts. Insists on Puritan position that marriage is higher state than celibacy; husbands should not beat wives; should be no marriage without betrothal or after "deflowering." Influential treatise, especially in America, where his belief that divorce was possible for more reasons than adultery became basis of more liberal separation positions.

Phaer, Thomas. *The Boke of Chyldren.* 1544.*
Considered first book on pediatrics, rare in time when childcare information was usually appended to midwifery books. Appears as part of Jehan Goeurot's *The Regiment of Lyfe,* 2nd through 9th editions. Phaer was translator of Goeurot's work.

Pinchbeck, Ivy and Margaret Hewitt. *Children in English Society: From Tudor Times to the Eighteenth Century.* London: Routledge & K. Paul, 1969.
See page 44 for legal ages for betrothal and marriage.

Platt, Hugh. *Delightes for Ladies, to Adorne their Persons, Tables, Closets, and Distillatories.* [1600?]**
Popular book on housewifery with decorative borders on tiny pages.

Pollard, A. W. and G. R. Redgrave. *A Short-Title Catalogue of Books Printed in England, Scotland and Ireland . . .1475–1640.* 2nd edition, revised. 3 Vols. London: Bibliographical Society, 1976.
Basic bibliography. *See* Wing for 1640–1700 publications.

Popular Culture in Seventeenth-Century England. London: Routledge, 1988. Edited by Barry Reay. Reprint of first edition published by Croom Helm, 1985.
See especially "The Reform of Popular Culture? Sex and Marriage in Early Modern England" and "Ridings, Rough Music and Mocking Rhymes in Early Modern England," both by Martin Ingram, pages 129–97. The latter describes community "Ridings" to ridicule husbands whose wives dominate them.

Powell, Thomas. *Tom of All Trades, Or the Plaine Path-way to Preferment.* 1631.*
Advice on various professions and marriage partners and training for each.

Primaudaye, Peter de la. *See* La Primaudaye.

Quaife, G. R. *Wanton Wenches and Wayward Wives: Peasants and Illicit Sex in Early Seventeenth-Century England.* New Brunswick, N.J.: Rutgers Univ. Press, 1979.
Good descriptions of families of yeomen, husbandmen, and laborers, as well as views of marriage by lower gentry and peasantry.

Quennell, Marjorie and C. H. B. *A History of Everyday Things in England 1066–1799.* 2nd edition. London: B. T. Batsford, 1930.
Comments and illustrations on everything from castles, costumes, and food to ships, coaches, and armour. Several other editions from 1918 to 1950. *See also* Trevelyan.

Rabisha, William. *The Whole Body of Cookery Dissected.* 1675.
Recipes plus description of a "great feast made ... in the days of Edward the fourth" with a list of those in attendance.

Rich, Barnabe. *The Honestie of this Age.* 1614.*
Moral discourse including belief that female blushing is sign of chaste mind.

_____. *My Ladies Looking Glasse.* 1616.
Treatise on sins of both men and women. Earlier 1606 version called *Faultes. See* Hull for more books by Rich addressed to female audience.

Riddle, John M. *Contraception and Abortion from the Ancient World to the Renaissance.* Cambridge, Mass.: Harvard Univ. Press, 1992.

Roesslin, Eucharius. *The Byrth of Mankynde.* 1540.**
Earliest midwifery book in English; translated from Latin. Later editions extended title to say, "Otherwyse Named the Womans Booke." Includes illustrations.

Rogers, Daniel. *Matrimonial Honor.* 1642.*

[Roxburghe] Society, The. *Roxburghe Ballads.* 3 vols. Hertford: Steven Austin for the Ballad Society, 1871–1899.
Multivolume collection of old English ballads with drawings/illustrations.

Rüff, James. *The Expert Midwife.* 1637.
Translation from Latin for women so they may know better how to handle childbirth problems, though such knowledge might take business away from men. Illustrations.

Russell, Josiah Cox. *British Medieval Population.* Albuquerque: Univ. of New Mexico Press, 1948.

Sadler, John. *The Sicke Womans Private Looking-Glasse.* 1636.
Subtitle is "Wherein methodically are handled all uterine affects, or diseases arising from the womb enabling women to inform the physician about the cause of their griefe."

Salter, Thomas. *A Mirrhor Mete for all Mothers, Matrones, and Maidens, Intituled The Mirrhor of Modestie.* 1579.
Severely restrictive instructions for girls and women; translation of Bruto (*see*).

Schofield, Roger and E. A. Wrigley. "Infant and Child Mortality in England in the Late Tudor and Early Stuart Period." *Health, Medicine and Mortality in the Sixteenth Century.* Edited by Charles Webster. Cambridge: Univ. Press, 1979. 61–95.

Sharp, Jane. *The Midwives Book: or the Whole Art of Midwifry.* 1671.*
Reprinted through 1728. Now available from Providence: Brown Univ.,
Women Writers Project.

First English midwifery book by a woman. Text includes common misconceptions and frank description of sex organs. See pages 47–54 of James Aveling's *English Midwives* (1872, 1967) for limited excerpts, and Elaine Hobby's *Virtue of
Necessity* (185–87) and Hilda Smith's *Reason's Desciples* (97–102) for discussions
of Sharp.

*Silent but for the Word: Tudor Women as Patrons, Translators, and Writers of
Religious Works.* Edited by Margaret Hannay. Kent, Ohio: Kent State
Univ. Press, 1985.

Slater, Miriam. *Family Life in the Seventeenth Century: The Verneys of Claydon
House.* London and Boston: Routledge and Kegan Paul, 1984.

See page 62 for explanation of financial settlements connected with marriage
(e.g. portion, jointure). Letters describe attempts to "place out" children with
relatives.

Smith, Hilda L. *Reason's Disciples: Seventeenth-Century English Feminists.*
Urbana: Univ. of Illinois, 1982.

See pages 97–102 for discussion of attempts by Jane Sharp, Elizabeth Cellier, and
Hannah Wolley to improve midwifery education in seventeenth century.

Sowernam, Esther [pseud.]. *Esther Hath Hang'd Haman: or an Answere to a
Lewd Pamphlet . . .* 1617.

Response to Swetnam. *See* Henderson and McManus for partial text and precis.

Speght, Rachel. A Mouzell for Melastomus . . . 1617.

Response to Swetnam. *See* Henderson and McManus for partial text and precis.

Spufford, Margaret. "The Schooling of the Peasantry in Cambridgeshire 1575–
1700." *Land, Church, and People.* Edited by Joan Thirsk. Welwyn Garden
City, Hertfordshire: British Historical Society, 1970. 112–47.

———.*Small Books and Pleasant Histories: Popular Fiction and Its Readership
in Seventeenth-Century England.* Athens: Univ. of Georgia, 1982.

See pages 19–44 for reading instruction for girls.

Stenton, Doris Mary. *The English Woman in History.* London: George Allen &
Unwin; New York: Macmillan, 1957.

Useful, pre-"women's movement" history of English women. See chapters 4, 5, 6.

Stevenson, Kenneth. *Nuptial Blessing: A Study of Christian Marriage Rites.* London: Alcuin Club, 1982.

See page 135 for wording of marriage vows.

Strangehopes, Samuel. *A Book of Knowledge.* 1675.*

Medicinal recipes.

Stubbes, Philip. *A Christal Glasse for Christian Women.* 1591.**

Bestseller by husband of pious woman who died after childbirth. Praises her for study of scriptures, her silence, fact that she stayed at home and learned from her husband.

Swetnam, Joseph. *The Arraignment of Lewde, Idle, Froward, and Unconstant Women . . .* 1615.**

Popular attack on women, renewing "Controversy over Women." *See* Sowernam, Speght, and Munda for responses. *See also Half Humankind* by Henderson and McManus for partial text and precis.

Taylor, John. *The Needles Excellency.* 1631.*

Book of needlework designs prefaced by poem and drawing extolling use of sharp needle instead of sharp tongue.

———. *Wit and Mirth.* 1626.*

One of Taylor's many clever jest books, this one touching on female failings. Taylor was the popular and prolific "water-poet," so called because he was trained as a waterman.

Temple, Dorothy (Osborne), Lady (1627–1694). *The Letters of Dorothy to William Temple.* Edited by G. C. Moore Smith. Oxford: Clarendon Press, 1928.

Correspondence with her future husband, William Temple. Letters 36 and 37 tell of reading and sharing French romances with Sir William. She reads in French and is critical of English translations.

Thompson, Roger. *Women in Stuart England and America: A Comparative Study.* London and Boston: Routledge & Kegan Paul, 1974.

Includes population and sex ratio information.

Thornton, Alice. *The Autobiography of Mrs. Alice Thornton of East Newton, Co. York.* Durham: Andrews & Co., 1875.

Describes physical ailments and misfortunes she endured over many years. Excerpts in *By a Woman Writt.* First published long after her death in 1706/7.

Tilney, Edmund. *A Brief and Pleasant Discourse of Duties in Marriage called . . . The Flower of Friendshippe.* 1568.*
Popular marriage guide; discusses and rejects possibility of equality between men and women on earth.

Todd, Edwin M. *Reflections Through a Murky Crystal.* Pasadena, Calif.,1986.
Brief essays on medical history by a modern doctor with comments on early physicians.

Treasury of Hidden Secrets, The, Commonly Called the Good-Huswives Closet of Provision for the Health of Her Houshold. 1659.
Subtitle says, "gathered out of sundry experiments, lately practised by men of great knowledge." Similar to Partridge (*see*).

Trevelyan, G. M. *Illustrated English Social History: Volume Two: The Age of Shakespeare and the Stuart Period.* London: Longmans, Green, 1942.
Helpful guide to everyday life in the Tudor-Stuart period. *See also* Quennell.

Tuke, Thomas. *A Discourse Against Painting and Tincturing of Women.* 1616.
Criticism of unnatural look achieved with cosmetics. According to Crawford bibliography (*see*), this work was translated by a woman, Elizabeth Arnold.

Tusser, Thomas. *Five Hundreth Points of Good Husbandry United to as Many of Good Huswiferie.* 1573. *See Daughters, Wives, and Widows* for excerpts.
Popular rhymed household guide, sequel to *A Hundrethe Good Pointes. . .*(1557). Householders' chores arranged by months; a kind of almanac.

Tuvil, Daniel. *Asylum Veneris or a Sanctuary for Ladies.* 1616.
Compares women (particularly "their abilities and graces") favorably with men.

Tyler, Margaret. *See* Ortunez de Calahorra.

Ulrich, Laura Thatcher. *A Midwife's Tale.* New York: Knopf, 1990.
Statistics on maternal deathrate in childbirth in England and New England.

_____. *Good Wives: Image and Reality in the Lives of Women in Northern New England: 1650–1750.* New York: Knopf, 1982.

Underdowne, Thomas. *The Excellent Historye of Theseus and Ariadne.* 1566.
Short rhymed story with harsh introduction suggesting (facetiously?) that daughters "going abroad" have their legs broken.

Vaughan, Robert. *A Dyalogue Defensyve for Women agaynst Melycyous Detractoures.* 1542.
Lengthy dialogue between two birds arguing merits and imperfections of women.

Verney, Margaret M. *Memoirs of the Verney Family During the Commonwealth, 1650–1660: Compiled from the Letters and Illustrated by the Portraits at Claydon House.* London: Longmans, Green and Co., 1894.

"Virgin's A.B.C." *Roxburghe Ballads.* Vol. 2, Pt. 3: 650.
Alphabetical, rhymed prescriptions for young girl's life.

Vives, Juan Luis. *The Instruction of a Christen Woman.* [1529?].*
Facsimile reprint in Diane Bornstein. *Distaves and Dames.* Delmar, N.Y.: Scholars' Facsimiles & Reprints, 1978. *See also* Foster Watson, *Vives and the Renascence Education of Women.* London: Edward Arnold, 1912.

Guide to raising daughters by adviser to Catherine of Aragon.

von Baer, Karl Ernst. *See* Baer.

Warnicke, Retha M. *Women of the English Renaissance and Reformation.* Westport, Conn.: Greenwood Press, 1983.

Wertz, Richard W. and Dorothy C. *Lying-In: A History of Childbirth in America.* New York: Shocken Books, 1979.
More about midwives and birth rites.

Whately, William. *A Bride-Bush, or a Wedding Sermon.* 1617.*
Whately, a preacher, was an early exponent of divorce and remarriage in case of desertion, but he was forced to back down in later editions.

Wilkinson, Robert. *The Merchant Royall.* 1607.*
Marriage sermon with emphasis on role and duties of the wife.

Williamson, George, Dr. *Lady Anne Clifford, Countess of Dorset, Pembroke and Montgomery 1590–1676: Her Life, Letters and Work . . . .* Kendal: Titus Wilson, 1922.
Limited edition of 250; large book with many black-and-white illustrations.

Willoughby Letters. *See* Alice T. Friedman.

Wing, Donald. *Short-Title Catalogue of Books Printed in England, Scotland, Ireland, Wales, and British America and of English Books Printed in Other Countries 1641–1700.* 2nd edition revised, Vol. 1, A–England, 1994, and 2nd edition, Vols. 2 and 3. New York: Modern Language Association, 1988.
Basic bibliography, sequel to Pollard and Redgrave (*see*).

Winter, Salvator. *Directions for the Use of My Elixir . . .*1664.
Eight-page booklet extolling the virtues of his elixir, which, he claimed, "is sufficient not only to cure any disease incident unto man and to prolong even old age
itself but to prevent any disease from fixing upon you."

_____. *A New Dispensatory of Fourty Physical Receipts.* 1649.*
Fifteen pages of short narrative cures plus three "pleasant arts for young
gentlemen."

_____. *A Pretious Treasury: or a New Dispensatory.* 1649.
One of several 1649 books of remedies. Winter claims to be able to pull teeth
almost painlessly and "set in artificial ones that they shall not be discerned from
the natural ones" (p.15). Francis Dickinson and Winter are each an author of one
section of this pamphlet, which includes the quack medicine cartoon reproduced
in this book. *See* Dickinson with similar title, also printed in 1649.

Wolley, Hannah [?]. *The Accomplished Ladies Delight.* 1675.
This work and two other books, *The Gentlewomans Companion* (1673) and *The
Compleat Servant-Maid* (1677), were falsely attributed to Wolley, according to
Hobby, pages 166–77. This one included section on fishing and more orderly
arrangement of contents than was Wolley's wont. *The Gentlewomans Companion*
includes section on female education and improvements needed, but was apparently by a man.

Wolley, Hannah. *The Ladies Directory.* 1661.*
Wolley was the first woman to make a successful career of writing household
directories. This was her first of at least five popular books, the others being *The
Cooks Guide* (1664), *The Ladies Delight* (1672), *The Queen-like Closet* (1670), and
A Supplement to the Queenlike Closet (1674). *See* Hobby for in-depth discussion of
Wolley and her mimickers in last quarter of seventeenth century.

Women as Mothers in Pre-Industrial England. Edited by Valerie Fildes. London:
Routledge, 1990.
Seven essays; see especially pages 68–107 by Adrian Wilson on rituals of child-
birth, lying in, churching, separation of sexes, female culture.

Women in English Society 1500–1800. Edited by Mary Prior. New York:
Methuen, 1985.
Valuable essays including "Marital Fertility and Lactation 1570–1720" by
Dorothy McLaren and "Women's Published Writings 1600–1700" by Patricia
Crawford.

Women in the Renaissance: Selections from English Literary Renaissance. Edited by Kirby Farrell, Elizabeth H. Hageman, and Arthur F. Kinney. Amherst: Univ. of Massachusetts Press, 1990.

A dozen useful articles plus Hageman's excellent updated, annotated bibliography.

Wood, Owen. *An Alphabetical Book of Physical Secrets.* 1639.*

Long title directs work "most especially [to] householders in the country who are either farre remote or else not able to entertaine a learned physician: as likewise for the help of such Ladies and Gentlewomen who of charity labour to doe good."

Woodbridge, Linda. *Women and the English Renaissance: Literature and the Nature of Womankind 1540–1620.* Urbana and Chicago: Univ. of Illinois Press, 1984.

Looks at Renaissance women through various literary genres. Includes bibliography of primary and secondary sources.

Wright, Louis B. *Middle-Class Culture in Elizabethan England.* Ithaca, N.Y.: Cornell Univ. Press, 1965. 1st edition 1935.

Wrightson, Keith. *English Society 1580–1680.* London: Hutchinson, 1982.

Includes contraception practices, and views of marriage (gentry to peasant), infant care, and death.

Wrigley, E. A. "A Simple Model of London's Importance in Changing English Society and Economics 1650–1750." *Past and Present.* 37:44–46.

Statistics on population. Wrigley's figures are quoted in Roger Thompson's *Women in Stuart England and America.*

Wrigley, E. A. and R. S. Schofield. *The Population History of England 1541–1871.* Cambridge, Mass.: Harvard Univ. Press, 1981.

Youngs, Frederic A. *The Proclamations of the Tudor Queens.* Cambridge: Univ. Press, [1976].

See pages 161–70 for proclamations on apparel whose purpose was to identify each rank of society by clothing worn. ❦

Index